LIFE IN A WEEK

Life in a Week

A Journey to Happiness and Spiritual Awakening

MICHAEL SHAWN KELLER

Your Time, LLC

Life in a Week – 2nd Edition

A Journey to Happiness and Spiritual Awakening

Michael Shawn Keller

Dedication

To those who dare to dream, embrace change, and relentlessly pursue personal growth, may this book serve as a guiding light on your journey to becoming the best version of yourself.

Also, to our son Jack Alexander Keller Orellana who inspires us to grow and learn each day along with him.

Love always,
Dad and Papi

Forward

In a world that seems to accelerate endlessly, where time is both our greatest asset and our most elusive pursuit, finding meaning, happiness, and a deeper connection to our own spirits can often feel like a huge challenge. Yet, nestled within the pages of this book, you hold the keys to unlocking a timeless journey—a journey to happiness and spiritual awareness that has the power to transform your life in the span of a mere week.

"Life in a Week - 2nd Edition: A Journey to Happiness and Spiritual Awakening" stands as a beacon of wisdom and guidance in simple words, beckoning to all those who seek a life with fulfillment, simplicity, and profound awareness. This edition is a continuation of the trailblazing path set forth by its predecessor, the work penned by me, Michael Keller in 2009. My first endeavor sought to aid those yearning for a more meaningful existence—a mission I now carry forward with renewed depth and insight from more years of an amazing life.

In this age of noise and distraction, where modernity often drowns out the whispers of our own souls, the words contained within these pages are a call to reconnect with our essence. Drawing upon years of wisdom gained through introspection, experience, studying some of the most spiritual teachings, and a profound commitment to understanding the human condition, I present a refined roadmap for embarking on a transformative journey.

This journey is not a mere collection of steps and rituals, but a simple approach to life—a celebration of the profound beauty hidden within the mundane, the sacredness inherent in the everyday. Through carefully crafted exercises, heartfelt reflections, and poignant anecdotes, I will try to guide us through the labyrinth of our thoughts, emotions, and aspirations, unveiling our own existence and illuminating the path towards self-discovery.

As we embark on this journey, we are invited to shed the layers of societal conditioning, to strip away the noise that masks our true selves, and to rediscover the purity of our souls. The second edition of "Life in a Week" is not just a book; it is a timeless companion, a steadfast ally, and a reservoir of wisdom that beckons us to dance with life's rhythm, to savor its fleeting moments, and to embrace the profound interconnectedness that binds us all.

So, dear reader, take a leap of faith into these pages. Allow these simple and down to earth words to wash over you, like a gentle breeze carrying the scent of possibility. As you embark on this week-long journey to happiness and spiritual awareness, may you discover that the treasure you seek has been within you all along. May you find solace, inspiration, and the profound sense of belonging that comes from realizing your place in our existence together in this amazing thing we call life.

With anticipation and heartfelt blessings,

Michael Shawn Keller

Table of Contents

CHAPTER ONE: EVERYDAY LIFE

WILL THIS REALLY MATTER IN FIVE YEARS?

We live in a strange time and in a strange world. It's funny how we're all here on a planet that spins around the universe in circles nonstop. There are many worlds out there in many galaxies. There are billions of living creatures and life surrounding us, yet we get caught up in our own little worlds. We worry about some of the stupidest things, things that don't even matter, or things that will only happen in your own head because they simply will never actually happen.

We worry about money, popularity, cars, our shoes... whatever. It doesn't matter. Trust me when I say it doesn't matter. It's all an illusion made up in our own minds. We think so much about these worries, or illusions, that we create significant amounts of unnecessary stress. This stress will eventually turn into ulcers, premature aging, and sickness. Usually, when we get those symptoms, we will turn to negative outlets such as self-medication, alcohol, or overeating. Regardless of whatever outlet we choose to turn to, we will end up with the same result. That result is usually emptiness, sadness, or hatred.

We need to remember that there are some things that we cannot change, the sun goes down each night and then returns the next day and winter comes but spring will soon return. These are things that happen no matter what, we have been recording this for thousands of years so why do people get so stressed when winter comes, and the crops won't grow? What we can change though is our attitude or our thoughts. Nothing changes if we do not change. If you are unhappy with where you are at this time in your life but do nothing to change it then let me tell you where you will be in five years; yup, right where you are! I once told a co-worker don't work to expect only a paycheck, work on yourself and do all that you can to improve yourself and the work will flow to you, and you won't need to sweat 10 hours a day for simply a paycheck. He took my advice and started to learn everything he could about the trade we were working in and soon opened his own business which grew twice as large as the company we were working for at the time.

As soon as we realize that all those worries are just illusions within our own minds and that they really won't matter in the long run, it will be so much easier to just let them go. Let them roll right off your back. Every time something bothers me, I ask myself one simple question: "Will this really matter in five years?" If not, I let it go. After you do this a few times, it will become a habit, and you will see that these worries really will just roll off your back.

It took me a long time to figure out how to let go of everyday stress. For a long time, I would let things get to me and constantly worry about that driver who cut me off on my way to work, the phone bill that was due last week, or the kid at the coffee shop who didn't put cream in my coffee when I specifically asked for cream. The list could go on for pages. My mind was going all the time, screaming at me, and arguing with me to just stay mad because it is easier. The chatter in my head was so constant that I didn't have the time or energy to change my habits. If only I knew years ago that our thoughts create our realities, this simple fact can change anyone's life. What we focus on is attracted to us and what we think about will always become reality so remember to listen to your thoughts carefully and learn to re-think what you are concentrating on throughout the day.

We all have two voices in our heads. We are constantly talking to each of them. I know this sounds weird, but it is true. Let's take a few seconds and do this small test to help me to show you what

I mean. Stop reading for fifteen seconds, and just sit still and think about absolutely nothing. Okay, start now. Alright, you are back. Great! Did you have one voice tell you that this author doesn't know what he is talking about, that you don't have voices in your head? Meanwhile, did the other voice disagree with you and begin thinking about what you are going to cook for dinner or why the sky is blue? The voices just keep going and going. Sometimes when you are trying to fall asleep, they keep talking and asking you questions like "Did you call Madison back? Did you put the toilet seat down? I wonder how Jack is doing?" And they keep going and going. It's as if they just need to keep talking and going on about anything and everything (we all know someone like that too). Those voices or thoughts are normal and healthy if you can get them to be quiet when you want to fall asleep or relax. We let our minds chatter sometimes to distract us from the issues that bombard us all day at work, school, on the news, etc.

As we change the way we think and live in a more positive and loving way, all that chatter seems to quiet down automatically, and it turns into normal thoughts of the moment. When we learn to think and live in the moment and not in the past or in the future, but right now, life gets so much better and easier. This is a very difficult thing to do because we have EGO's and honestly, I think we may even like the drama when we focus on something in the past that we didn't like or stress about the worries of the future. Let me let you in on a small secret that took me well into my forties to figure out; most of the things we worry about will never happen so just let it go and enjoy the moment at hand. Of course, we should plan for tomorrows but just don't live there.

Life constantly changes every minute of every day, and that is a great thing. If it didn't change, we would live stale lives. If we live in the past, then we are missing out on the now. It is a wonderful thing to remember, rejoice in, and learn from the past, but it is a dangerous thing to stay there. The same goes with the future. We should save money and set goals for the future (envision them in detail and they will happen sooner than you imagine), but don't forget to enjoy the beautiful day outside today. I can see the beach from where I live, yet up until recently, I didn't get sand in my toes for a couple of years at a time. I didn't even think of taking walks to watch the sunrise or sunset because I was too busy trying to work on my future. I was so caught up in the future that I forgot about today. We cannot change our pasts, but we can start fresh today because it is a new day. Make dinner with your family and friends; it is fun when everyone gets involved in the cooking. Go to the park and go down the slide. Stay in tonight and watch a good movie. Do something, but just enjoy life today. We don't know what tomorrow will bring, but we do know that if we take time to enjoy today, tomorrow will only get better because of today.

The truth of the matter is time is our most precious gift, we can never know how long we have so don't waste it on foolish things that don't help you or your family or community, it is important to work and to earn money but do not let that be your only focus. We can never get time back. Image time as a precious resource that once it's used, you can't get it back. It's like sand slipping through your fingers – once it's gone, you can't put it back in the hourglass. Time is incredibly valuable because we have a limited amount of it in our lives. Just like you can't un-bake a cake, you can't undo the moments that have passed. That's why people say time is more valuable than anything else – you can't buy or make more of it. So, it's important to use your time wisely and cherish the moments you have.

LOVE LOVES COMPANY

The thoughts we feel are shown by our tone of voice, our facial expressions, and our body language. If we are thinking happy thoughts, then we will show happiness. If we are thinking negative or mean-spirited thoughts, we will show fear or negativity. Think about it. Here's a good example: my boss asked me if I would mind working on Saturday, but I had plans to go out to a show that day. Because I didn't want to let him down, I said, "Sure, no problem." He was able to easily pick up on my unspoken thoughts and responded by saying, "Thanks, Mike. I really appreciate you working. I can tell you have plans but are still willing to kick in on such short notice."

When our thoughts are filled with anger or fear, they dim the natural light of our hearts. Love is the natural light that brings us happiness, joy, peace, and health. Anger, hate, sadness, stress, and doubt are all the opposite of love; they are darkness. Darkness in the heart is natural poison, and it will kill us. When that natural poison is in our thoughts, it will show up in our body language, facial expressions, and tone of voice.

These expressions will attract the same in people around us. You know the old saying "misery loves company," well, that is true. The same is also true about love: "love loves company." Love is just as contagious as hate. Love is life. Love is what makes us happy and healthy.

A quick story about how I had anger built up in my heart. I worked for a company for many years, toward the end of my employment with the company things changed for the worse. My relationship with the owners became hindered because of circumstances that were beyond my control and I was fired from the company. I held onto anger and even disappointment over their actions until a few months later when I realized that I had no control over other people's motives or actions. For those few months that I held onto the anger, I felt tired and old. Then one day I realized it was a blessing in disguise because I was only living comfortably with a job that I had very little passion for. Even though that door closed, there were many better doors to walk through! I had started a side hustle a year earlier and now that side hustle became my new career at the time. So even though something seemed bad at the time, it was one of the best things that could have happened because I focused on me for the first time in a long while. My friends and family instantly noticed that my heart was freed from the shackles of anger, and I felt like I was a new man again, a man with unlimited goals and joys.

Everyone is here for a reason, and that reason is to express ourselves and bring happiness and joy to this world. When we have happy thoughts filled with love and goodness, it will radiate through us naturally in our voices, expressions, and our vibes. When I feel like I'm going to have a stressful day or a difficult time, I will. When I feel like it's going to be a great day filled with laughter, it will be. Our thoughts are what make us up; therefore, our thoughts are who we are. You can be the most handsome guy or the prettiest girl at the dance, but if you don't know it, it won't matter because you're not going to dance much. However, if you thought positively with love, then you would know what a hot ticket you really are, and you would have the confidence to ask anyone to dance. You would have a great time because love attracts love.

Love yourself for who you are, and you will be surrounded by love. Treat people with love, and most will respond likewise. If someone is mean-spirited to you when you were only good to them, don't let it bother you. If you let their negativity enter your thoughts, you are only giving that negativity power. What I do is simply walk away and wish that person goodwill and peace. If I can't just walk away due to circumstances, I will never react in the same negative way, no matter what. Always try to treat others how you would want to be treated. Do not treat others how they treat you. Maybe your smile or your brushing off of the rude words spoken to you will eventually plant a seed of goodness and love into the negative person's heart and, therefore, their thoughts.

When we walk around knowing we are good and helping everyone we can, we will radiate that love through our vibes, expressions, and body language; we will pass it along to everyone we meet. That happiness and love really is contagious, so hold that door open for the next person, say hello to the old guy on the park bench, ask the cashier how her day is going, and you will make a difference in someone else's day. That difference will not only be contagious to them, but also to you; your thoughts will stay more positive, therefore making your day better and healthier too.

Life can often be like a rollercoaster, full of twists, turns, and the occasional loop-de-loop. And just like any thrilling ride, it's easy to get caught up in the ups and downs, the highs and lows of everyday existence. But what if I told you that there's a way to navigate life's twists and turns with a big smile on your face, all while spreading love like confetti at a parade? That's right, it's time to embrace the spiritual and loving way of living, where love truly loves love, and stress is just a distant memory.

Imagine this: you wake up in the morning, and instead of groaning about the day ahead, you greet it with open arms and a heart full of love. Sounds too good to be true, right? Well, it's not. It all starts with understanding the power of unconditional love.

Unconditional love means loving without conditions or expectations. It's the kind of love that doesn't say, "I'll love you if you do this for me." No, it says, "I love you, no matter what." When you love unconditionally, you're like a beacon of light in the darkness, radiating love to everyone you encounter.

There's a saying that goes, "The words we utter are the truths to come." It's like a cosmic reminder that the things we speak into existence have a way of shaping our reality. So why not speak love into your life?

Picture this: You're stuck in traffic, and the cars are honking, tempers are flaring, and stress is mounting. Instead of joining the chaos, you take a deep breath and say to yourself, "I choose love. I choose to let go of this stress." And suddenly, the traffic doesn't seem as infuriating, and you find yourself humming your favorite tune, spreading love even in the midst of chaos.

Now, let's talk about the LoveFest of everyday life. You don't need to wait for a special event to celebrate love. Every day can be a LoveFest if you choose to see it that way.

Imagine this: You're at the grocery store, and someone accidentally bumps into your cart. Instead of reacting with irritation, you offer a warm smile and say, "No worries, it happens to the best of us." Suddenly, you've turned a potentially stressful situation into a moment of connection and love.

If you want to live through love and get rid of stress from your life, don't forget the magic of laughter. Laughter is like a universal language of love, and it's contagious in the best possible way.

Picture this: You're at work, and a colleague starts complaining about the never-ending emails and deadlines. Instead of commiserating, you break into a silly dance, and before you know it, your entire team is laughing together. The stress melts away, replaced by a sense of camaraderie and love.

In the end, the spiritual and loving way to live is all about embracing love as your guiding light. It's about choosing love over stress, spreading love through your words and actions, and celebrating love in the everyday moments of life. Remember, love loves love, and the more you give, the more you'll receive.

So, my fellow adventurers on this rollercoaster called life, let's embark on this hilarious and intense journey of living through love. Let's laugh in the face of stress, dance through the challenges, and remember that love is the ultimate truth we seek. And who knows, you might just find that life becomes a whole lot more fun when you let love lead the way.

The COVID-19 pandemic descended upon the world like an uninvited storm, disrupting lives, economies, and daily routines. While the virus itself posed a formidable threat, it was the isolation and separation it brought that tested the limits of human resilience. In the midst of this crisis, love emerged as a beacon of hope, saving countless lives in ways both extraordinary and ordinary.

For many seniors, the pandemic was a cruel twist of fate. Isolated in their homes, they found themselves cut off from the world, their beloved family and friends suddenly out of reach. But it was their neighbors and communities that stepped up to bridge the gap.

In neighborhoods across the globe, acts of love and kindness became a daily ritual. Seniors found bags of groceries and homemade meals left on their doorsteps, accompanied by heartfelt notes from caring neighbors who had become their lifelines. It wasn't just about sustenance; it was about the warmth of knowing that someone cared. It was about the human connection that transcended the physical distance.

Zoom calls and virtual gatherings became the norm. Families and friends who couldn't be together physically found new ways to connect. These digital lifelines became a testament to the enduring power of love. Grandparents met their newborn grandchildren through screens, and friends held virtual game nights, proving that love could conquer the barriers of distance.

Yet, the pandemic took a toll on mental health like never before. The isolation, uncertainty, and fear weighed heavily on people's minds. But once again, love came to the rescue.

Communities rallied to support those struggling with their mental health. Hotlines and support groups were established, offering a lifeline to those feeling overwhelmed. Neighbors checked in on each other, friends became confidants, and strangers became sources of comfort. The simple act of listening, of offering a shoulder to lean on, became an expression of love that saved lives.

In healthcare facilities, doctors, nurses, and medical staff faced the pandemic head-on. They worked long hours, often in grueling conditions, separated from their own families to care for the sick. Their commitment and sacrifice were a testament to the love they held for their patients and the communities they served.

The search for a vaccine was a testament to global cooperation and love for humanity. Scientists and researchers from different corners of the world shared knowledge and collaborated like never before. Love for one's fellow humans drove them to work tirelessly to find a solution to the crisis.

As the pandemic raged on, stories of love and courage emerged from every corner. Teachers who adapted to virtual classrooms, parents who juggled work and childcare, and essential workers who continued to serve their communities—all exhibited unwavering love for their fellow humans.

The COVID-19 pandemic was a test of humanity's resilience, and love emerged as the strongest force. It was the love that led neighbors to help neighbors, friends to support friends, and strangers to extend a hand in times of need. It was the love that saved lives, both physically and mentally. And as we emerged from the darkness of the pandemic, the lessons of love learned during this crisis would remain a beacon of hope for generations to come.

SECOND NATURE

Every single one of us is a creature of habit, both good and bad. Whether it's learning how to walk, drive a car, or cook a delicious dinner, it all becomes second nature to us simply by repeating habits. After a while, these habits become automatic to us. Every thought and emotion that we have, or feel is recorded in our subconscious mind, and if we think or feel these thoughts and emotions often enough, they will become habits. These habits will, in turn, become second nature.

We have the ability and strength to make choices every minute of our lives. By nature, we are strong, good, and loving. When we were little kids we only thought about the moment. Up until we are about four or five years old, we don't even understand the concept of time. As children, we didn't care about yesterday, and we were not concerned with tomorrow. That is why we naturally laughed at anything and everything at that age. We were not concerned that we only had one more hour at the party, we were too busy having fun now. When I watch kids play, it reminds me of those careless days without worries, problems, and stress. I watch children as they constantly laugh and play, without worrying about who has crooked teeth, a fat belly, or the expensive sweater on.

We learn everything by repeating it, by habit. It's the way we are built. We do things automatically all day long without even thinking about it; this is done by our second nature. Our second nature, or subconscious mind, knows the difference between good and bad; it naturally wants us to do the right and good thing, but our conscious mind is the final decision maker. Our conscious thinking throughout the day feeds our second nature (subconscious thinking). We give it information by our thoughts and actions. If you get up every morning for a year and have a cup of coffee, not only will you have that habit, but some mornings you will have finished the coffee before you even thought about having it.

I started to drink rum and coke socially when I was twenty-three years old. By the time I was thirty years old, many of my friends nicknamed me "the Captain" after the brand of rum that I drank. It was a habit I had to relax and socialize at the time. That habit became second nature to me. I automatically went home at the end of the day and made myself a drink. This turned into a really bad habit and a problem; I became what doctors would call a productive alcoholic. I went to work every morning and did a great job, spent time with my family and friends, and even went to the gym three times a week, but I was living in a fog.

I would tell myself that I was normal, that everyone had a few drinks after work every day. Because I told myself over and over that this was true, I believed it. This is the reality with everything in life. Think about it for a minute. If you look in the mirror when you feel down in the dumps about someone hurting your feelings, maybe your friend or sister said you look fat or that you have a big nose. Now you look in the mirror, and you will think "wow, I am fat" or "my nose is pretty big." That is because you have believed that to be true at some point in your life. It is an illusion that you believe to be true at that moment because you told yourself those horrible things over and over in the past. You can be ninety pounds and have the most petite nose in the world, but you told yourself those untruths in the past, and your second nature or subconscious mind recorded them and implanted them in your memory. Now the next day you find out that you got the promotion you've been working toward for a long time, and you happen to walk by that same mirror. This time, you stop and see the great person you really are. I constantly remind myself the thoughts I have are who I am. If I want to be that negative, grouchy fart in the office, all I have to do is think I am. Because I would much rather be that handsome, jolly guy, I remind myself how good I am by treating everyone with respect, by continuing to tell my corny jokes, and by having fun while I work – just like when I was a kid.

When I really wanted to stop drinking alcohol because I knew that it had become a big problem in my life and was causing major problems both physically and mentally, I tried everything. I tried to stop cold turkey, cut it down to just the weekends, and have only one after work. I would end up back where I started because it was second nature for me and because I had done it for so long. I tried reading books on the subject. I went to meetings and talked with my doctor, but I could not stop. I became so mad and disappointed in myself that I did not have the willpower to stop. Then one night as I was falling asleep, I remembered that "I am what I think I am." I was telling myself that I was powerless over alcohol and that I would never be able to stop drinking. My subconscious mind believed this to be true because I kept telling myself this, just like looking in that darn mirror again.

Every night before I fell asleep and every morning when I woke up, I would thank God for another day without alcohol, and I would repeat to myself that I don't want alcohol and that I don't even like alcohol anymore. By telling myself this every day and repeating this over and over to my second nature, or subconscious mind, I came to believe it and was able to change the bad habit. Another big key was figuring out why I was drinking so much, what in my life was making me want to numb my feelings with an addiction? I was fighting living my true life and simply living comfortably in my personal and professional life because it was easier just floating by in life. This was a huge mistake because I would never be able to live to my full potential and happiest. I will touch on this later in the book again because living life simply comfortably is not really living.

When we want to break a bad habit or start a good one, all we need to do is repeat it to ourselves over and over during the day and at night in our thoughts. It will become second nature in a very short time. Let your second nature take over the hard part and believe in yourself; it has worked for me when many believed I needed a miracle. Everything in our lives is caused by our own thoughts, our second nature, and our outlook on life. We will never be able to control the weather or other people, but if we make it a habit of believing in ourselves, laughing more often, and reminding ourselves of all our good habits, we will control our overall happiness and future.

MOVE THAT BODY

Have you ever noticed how great you feel after taking a walk, playing basketball, or even just shopping? It's a great feeling to move around and get our bodies going. Exercise is the natural way to let our positive feelings loose and to transform the moods we are in.

When I get in a grumpy mood, the first thing I do is to take a deep breath in and hold it for a few seconds, then I let it out slowly. I do this four or five times to get my lungs moving and to let the fresh air into my body while picturing the negativity flowing out of me with every exhale. This causes the endorphins in our bodies to begin to wake up and stretch. Now is the key time to take a quick walk even if it's just parking farther away from the building or store. Those few extra steps eventually add up and will give us an extra minute to just breathe and get more exercise.

Exercise promotes positive thinking because the more we exercise, the better we feel – both physically and mentally. The way we feel physically affects the quality of our lives. If we feel we can physically conquer issues in our lives, then we will know that we can do it mentally, too. It is really that simple. When I stopped drinking rum and colas every night and started to lose the second chin and the beach ball belly, I felt so much healthier. With this newfound extra energy and health, I started to do more at the gym. I lost about twenty-six pounds in four months without any real effort because I felt optimistic from feeling so great. I cannot stress how much work we do while exercising is mental and not physical.

The hardest part of going to the gym is the drive to the gym because we fill our thoughts with how tired we feel or how busy we are; therefore, even the drive is tiring. It is our thoughts that make us tired, so all we must do is change those thoughts of being tired into how much energy we have and how exercising will build up so much energy in us that we can even store some of that energy for the next trip to the gym. I found that cranking up the stereo in my car with upbeat music always helps me to stay motivated long enough to get me through the front door of the gym. Like I said, once we are in, it is easy!

Here is a quick story to help me to explain what I am talking about. Once upon a time, in a quaint little town, lived a woman named Grace. Grace was in her late 50s and had always been told that exercise was only for the young and physically fit. She felt discouraged and believed that she was too old and out of shape to make any significant changes to her health. But little did she know, a magical journey was about to unfold that would prove all her doubts wrong.

One bright sunny morning, Grace stumbled upon a dusty old book while cleaning her attic. The title caught her eye: "The Power of the Mind and the Law of Attraction." Curiosity piqued, she dusted off the cover and began to read. As she delved deeper into the book's teachings, she discovered the incredible concept that our thoughts could shape our reality.

The idea seemed too good to be true, but Grace decided to give it a try. She thought to herself, "What if age and shape don't really matter when it comes to improving my health and fitness? What if I can become healthier simply by thinking my way to a better life?"

With newfound hope, Grace set out on her journey to prove the power of her mind. She began with small steps. Even when working at her desk, she took regular breaks to stretch her body. At first, it was challenging, and her body protested against the unfamiliar movements. But she persisted, telling herself that every stretch brought her closer to better health.

As days turned into weeks, Grace noticed subtle changes. She felt more energetic, her joints were less stiff, and she found herself breathing easier. The Law of Attraction was starting to work its magic. Encouraged by her progress, Grace decided to take things a step further.

She started incorporating short walks into her daily routine, admiring the beauty of nature as she strolled through the park. Each step filled her with gratitude for her body and the opportunity to improve her well-being. As she walked, she imagined herself getting healthier and stronger with every stride.

To complement her newfound activity, Grace began to eat more mindfully, choosing healthier and nutritious options that fueled her body. She visualized her cells thriving with vitality and her muscles growing stronger. Everything we think turns into a feeling or an emotion that we have, and if we have those feelings enough, they become second nature. This is true with the feelings we have while we are exercising and even more so with the outcome of how we feel about ourselves and our bodies. The healthier our bodies are the better our self-esteem will be.

Stress is what gives us wrinkles, weak hearts, and anxiety. What we forget though, is that stress is the body's way of telling us to take a deep breath, slow down, laugh, and love. Most problems are built up in our own heads; they are mostly illusions made larger by our thoughts to help cope with everyday life. Sometimes we just need a little kick in the butt to remind us that all that worrying about the bills, the car, or the job is not going to help the situation. Negative thoughts create negative results. That's a fact. Let's stop stressing out on the issues and start focusing on what is important in life: our health, our energy, and our love for each other. Without them, we cannot accomplish anything, so take a few minutes to get fresh air and move around. Spend the time you deserve and need for yourself. You will be happier and less stressed, and life will be that much better.

I used to work tirelessly at a job that I thought was my only career path. It consumed so much of my time and energy for years, leaving little room for anything else. But then, life took an unexpected turn, and I got fired. It felt like a huge setback at first, but it turned out to be the wake-up call I needed. It made me realize that time is our most precious asset, and I had been squandering it on something that wasn't truly fulfilling. After some soul-searching, I decided to change my perspective and prioritize what truly mattered. Instead of just chasing after money or following people I did not truly respect, I focused on how I could make a positive impact on others' lives and build a better future for my family. It was like a weight was lifted off my shoulders, and now I feel more fulfilled and purposeful than ever before. It's amazing how a setback can lead to such a positive transformation, isn't it?

A simple truth I learned years ago is that when we chase money or anything for that matter, we are doing just the opposite of what we are trying, once we start being grateful for what we have we will attract more of what we have and will be blessed with abundance. Gratitude is the main key in everything, then envisioning it, and feeling the emotions of having it before you even get it. Everything in life is created twice, first in our thoughts and then into reality. So be very mindful of your thoughts because they do create your reality.

CHAPTER TWO: SPIRIT

FOUNDATIONS

Life is full of what we put out there. Whether it's happiness, love, and satisfaction or emptiness, loneliness, and sadness, it is all up to us. It's really pretty simple. It's like the old saying "you made your bed, now you have to lie in it." If you feel that you cannot trust people, you probably won't. If you feel like the world is against you, it probably will be. If you feel like everything is good and will work out for the best, it will. I truly believe in manifestation through our conscious and our subconscious and our thoughts, I watch my thoughts very carefully. It takes the tough times to know the good times. If we didn't have the tough times, then we would naturally forget how valuable the good times are and take them for granted. When you crush your finger between the balls at duckpin bowling and get a huge, throbbing blister on your finger that hurts every time you even get close to touching it, you will realize how lucky you always were when it wasn't hurt and how much you will appreciate it in a few days when it is healed.

When we realize that we really shouldn't try to change other people's habits or ways of thinking, but only change our own, it will have great rewards in all our relationships. We can always lead by example and actions, but we should never try to lecture and criticize others, even if it is the easy way out. Lecturing is one of the most destructive patterns we can have, and it will always end up with the same end result: resentment. Also, whatever change we were hoping for will be lost. Eventually, the person you are lecturing will reach the point of not even wanting to change and will start to look for your flaws instead. The love and respect that was once there will start to turn into more and more arguments; fighting will become a nasty habit or even the rule rather than the exception to the rule.

In all relationships, it is important to have trust and respect for each other, whether it is your spouse, kids, boss, or friends. It is so important to trust, and the easiest way to trust others is to trust yourself first. If you don't lie or cheat, then chances are people won't lie and cheat with you because they respect you. A perfect example of this would be a mother who is cleaning up a little in her sixteen-year-old son's bedroom and stumbles across some love letters sitting out in the open from a girl in his class. The mother is so tempted to read these letters to see what her son and this girl are up to, figuring that it can't hurt because no one would ever know that she snooped in her son's room. Later that day, she and her son are driving out to pick up some Chinese food for dinner, and her son comes right out and says to his mom with a huge smile, "Thanks for not reading those letters in my room when you were straightening up today. It really means a lot to me that you trust me." That mother just won some major trust with her son at a tough age, and he will feel so much more comfortable talking to his mom about his personal feelings and emotions because she gave him the trust he was trying so hard to get.

Let's face it: we are all pretty much bad actors. If she had read those letters and found something out that her son was hiding or didn't want her to know about, she would need to be a pretty good actor to not slip up and let him know that she knows what she read in those letters, or she would need to tell him that she went into his room, opened the letters, and snooped through his personal things. Of course, that would not create good feelings because it would show him that his mother did not trust him enough to leave the letters alone. Trust me when I say that she will find out and know one thousand times more about her son because she made the right choice and trusted him.

The trust and respect that this son and his mother share is the same foundation that all relationships are built on whether it is at home, with friends, or at work. It is like building your home on sand and hoping that the tide won't wash it into the ocean; eventually, that house will be washed away. Let's try and trust one another and build that house with a concrete foundation so that when the wind and waves get severe, it will be strong enough to withstand anything, even the biggest blizzard! My husband always says, "don't be looking for something that you didn't lose." Simply stating don't look for something because once you start looking or doubting you will always find something simply because you are hoping or searching for anything out of thin air.

If you start a relationship with lies and deception, it will always be strained with the fear of being lied to or deceived. If you feel like you cannot trust someone, you will eventually find yourself looking outside of that relationship for the comfort, care, and understanding you deserve. You will spend less time together and start spending more time on less important things. You will start to lose interest in what is really important to you: a relationship that should be filled with love and peace. The key is to be honest, even if it is hard because you feel like someone won't accept you or love you for who you are or because you are not perfect.

Allow me to let you in on a little secret: NO ONE is perfect, not even close to it. Everyone has good and bad moments; the key is to learn from both the good and bad moments and to move forward, making more of the good ones. Be honest all the time, and you will never have to worry about someone catching you in a lie. Be sincere all the time, and you will never have to wonder if you did your best. Never have regrets about what would have been because they are not. Be where you are at and move on. Make it good now. It may sound pretty hard, but it isn't. It's just being a good person, being honest, and building a solid foundation in all your relationships.

If you're starting a relationship and are worried that your partner won't love you because you snore awfully loud or because your feet sweat at night when you have blankets over them, then you won't be able to put all your energy into building the foundation necessary for the relationship to get to the point where he or she will find out about your horrible sounding snores or wet feet. If you know that no one is perfect, that those imperfections are part of who we are, and that it's okay to just be yourself, then you are building a strong foundation. The ironic part of it all is that if the person truly loves you, then he or she won't be bothered by the imperfections. Instead, he or she may even find those snores comforting and those damp feet to be romantic.

THE JUDGE

Life can be pretty stressful at times, especially when we get caught up in everyday worries. However, it becomes even more stressful when we have a bigger problem, a problem we have no authority or power over. The easiest way to turn that problem into a mountain when it originally started out as an anthill of a problem is by judging. Judging one another and ourselves is not only dangerous, but it is wrong.

The old saying "one should never throw stones when he himself lives in a glass house" is so simple and to the point. One would think that we generally practice this in our day-to-day lives but think about it for a minute. Here is a perfect example of a judgement that I recently made. I own a small janitorial company and when I arrived at the office to give an estimate for a move in cleaning there were three people there that I introduced myself to and asked to be shown around the office. I assumed that the older well-dressed person was the one I needed to get a quote out to and asked for his email. Come to find out the guy that was in his early twenties, dirty clothes, and changing light fixtures was the President and owner. I assumed it to be the well-dressed middle-aged man when all along it was the young hustler who was getting his hands dirty and sweating.

I have been practicing catching myself every time that I begin to judge someone else. At first, I could not believe how much I did it. I was shocked and would have never thought that it was an everyday occurrence. Try it for a couple of days, and I promise you that not only will you be shocked, but you will also have fun with it and learn something about yourself that you didn't know before. You will realize that you subconsciously judge others because of situations that have happened to you or that you have seen in your own life. For example, what do you think about the following descriptions as you read them: the kid with the blue Mohawk haircut, the heavy girl with the tight spandex pants, the thirty-year-old ringing up your burger at the drive-through, the guy with the black eye sitting next to you on the train? Now did you have a judgement for any of those people: Did you have a story made up in your head about any of them? Did you think anything negative about any of them? If so, let me remind you that every single one of them has their own story to tell about their life and their own unique personality. I would bet a large coffee that you probably were not even close to figuring them out at that first glance. I can also bet you that if you took the time to get to know any of them, there is a good chance that you would get along fine and maybe even become friends.

A big problem that we all have is that we take those initial two to eight seconds upon seeing someone and make that first impression judgement. This is natural and is mainly because we are human. It is also a protective sense that we use subconsciously to analyze any potential harm. But if there is no harm, then why we need to hold on to that judgement? Haven't we all gone to the store with messy hair, dirty clothes, or smelling a little ripe from a hard day's work?

I have learned that the less I judge others, the less I will be judged. Wouldn't it be a better world if we stopped judging and stopped the hate? There is no excuse for not liking someone because of their race, color, religious beliefs, or even hair style. I really believe that when we condemn others for who they are, it will all come back against us. We should remember to forgive others, and I don't just mean our family and friends. It is easy to forgive someone you love. I am talking about the person who cut you off on the road, the person who stole your wallet in Vegas, the person who called you a sour name, and even the person who may have hurt you deeply.

Two wrongs never make it right; such an act only puts you on the same level of thinking as the person who first wronged you.

There is a difference between judging a person and judging their actions. When I start to say or think something negative about something someone has done wrong, I have a habit of catching myself and start over. For example, if I were to call someone a jerk, I would catch myself and say "He is really acting like a jerk right now" instead. This way I am never judging another person, only their actions. Did you know that "pretty people" have a better chance of getting a new job than an "average looking person" according to a large study done by Yale? This is a perfect example of judging that we are discussing.

As I spoke about earlier in the book, losing my job after investing 24 years of my life into it was an incredibly disheartening experience. This role had become more than just a profession; it had woven itself into the fabric of my personal life as well. The colleagues I had worked with had become friends, and the challenges and victories we faced together had shaped my identity. When the news of my termination hit, I was overwhelmed with a mix of emotions, dominated by profound sadness and a sense of loss. However, as time went on, I realized that holding onto anger and resentment would only prolong my suffering. It wasn't an easy journey, but I made a conscious choice to forgive my former employer and not let this event define my worth. By choosing not to judge them and maintaining my sense of self-worth, I discovered an unexpected freedom. The burden of anger began to lift, making room for acceptance and new opportunities. This experience taught me that while the job was a significant part of my life, it wasn't the only defining aspect. Through forgiveness and self-compassion, I found the strength to move forward with grace and optimism, leaving behind the weight of bitterness and embracing the possibility of a brighter future.

When we bottle up anger and resentments, they will only grow and they will hurt us, causing more problems. The minute I realized

I was being foolish and that what was done was done, I felt a huge weight lift off my shoulders. I was no longer carrying around all the anger that was wasting so much of my energy.

Forgiveness is a transformative act that allows us to truly embrace life to its fullest. When we choose to forgive, we release the grip of anger and resentment that can otherwise consume us. Holding onto these negative emotions only serves to keep us trapped in a cycle of pain, restricting our potential for growth and happiness. By extending forgiveness and harboring well wishes for those who have wronged us, we set ourselves free from the burden of negativity.

Forgiveness doesn't mean excusing or forgetting what happened; it means liberating ourselves from the emotional shackles that tie us to the past. When we forgive, we create space for positivity to enter our lives. This act of letting go is like opening a window to allow fresh air and light to flood in. By releasing our grip on anger, we make room for healing, personal development, and new opportunities. Furthermore, the act of forgiving sends out a powerful message to the universe. When we choose to wish well for those who have hurt us, we shift our focus from dwelling on negativity to envisioning a brighter future. The energy we project into the world is one of openness and positivity, and this often attracts better circumstances and people into our lives. By choosing forgiveness over bitterness, we align ourselves with a path of growth and attract the positivity we deserve.

In the end, forgiveness is not just a gift we give to others, but a profound gift we give to ourselves. It's a conscious decision to break free from the chains of resentment and embrace a life that is rich with possibility and joy.

FORGIVE

We all have been misled, lied to, cheated, and hurt by someone at some time in our lives. Unfortunately, this is part of life. Like I said earlier, we are all good by nature, but we are blessed with free will, and sometimes we may take the rockier paths in life. That rocky road is full of hills, puddles, ditches, and even cliffs that sometimes cause us to fall or get wet. It is in our nature to do well, and if we aren't doing so well, we tend to try to cover up those shortcomings with deceptions. It feels horrible to be lied to or to be cheated, but there is always a positive lesson to be learned from every situation.

Every leader in every religion will tell you that it is key to forgive those who have wronged you. Did you know that there are 72 names for God throughout religions and languages? The bible says to forgive others so that you will be forgiven. Your gift will return to you in full, pressed down and shaken together to make room for more. The amount you give will determine the amount you get back. I believe those words and try to live by them every day because if you can't forgive, why in the world do you think anyone will ever forgive you when you screw up?

"A friend in need is a friend indeed" is another great old saying. Isn't that the truth? I have great friends who would do anything to help me – and have. I have been through some wonderful times and have had some tough times, but I have always had friends and family by my side through it all. I know that I can do or say things without thinking first or forget to ask how someone's day is when he or she really wanted me to be there.

The key to true friendship and love is being sincere and being honest enough to say you are sorry or that you were wrong. When you say you are sorry, you must really mean it. I screw up a lot, but I try my best to be a good person and admit when I am wrong. That's why it is so easy for me to accept an apology from others when they say or do something unkind to me. I look at it like this: we all wipe our butts the same way. All that means is we are all equal; no one is better than anyone else.

One day at a local market, a shopper found himself frustrated by the unfamiliar accents and customs of the immigrant vendors. Impatiently, he snapped at one vendor, making an insensitive comment about their way of doing things. Later, as he reflected on his behavior, he felt a pang of guilt. He realized he had unfairly judged and treated these individuals based on his limited perspective. Determined to make amends, he returned to the market the next day and approached the vendor he had offended. He admitted his mistake, expressing genuine remorse for his rude behavior. He then spent time conversing with the vendor, eager to learn about their culture, traditions, and way of life. Through this experience, he not only acknowledged his wrong actions but also embraced the opportunity to grow and appreciate the richness of diverse cultures. This story shows how forgiveness and learning starts with being able to notice we are the problem at times and that we must constantly remind ourselves that life is a learning journey together.

It hurts the most when someone close to you does something bad to you, and it will be the hardest to forgive that person because you have so much love for him or her. But you will feel so much more joy when you forgive that person because the burden was the heaviest when you were carrying it around with you, like a thirty-pound weight around your heart. Whenever we do something that will hurt someone we love, there is always a reason for doing it. Whether it was because we were only thinking about ourselves, we didn't think before we did it, or we just didn't care, there is always a reason. When we screw up, we really should figure out what the reason for the screw up was so that we don't do it again. If we excuse it again, then there is a problem because it's becoming a nasty habit. If someone hurts you and sincerely apologizes, it will be easy to forgive and forget. When it happens again, it won't be so easy.

That's when you really need to look at why they are doing what they are doing and ask yourself if you really want to be around a person at a time when your feelings aren't being considered. Whether you decide to walk away and take a break from the person who isn't concerned about your feelings, or you decide to try and work out the situation, always remember that all words spoken come from the heart. What you feel, what you desire, and what you love is spoken from the heart. When someone has a dimmed heart, it will show by their words and actions. When someone has a brightly lit heart, it will radiate through their words and actions. Therefore, if someone has negative things to say to you, they obviously feel those things in their heart.

I have found that when people enjoy picking on others, it's simply because they have low self-esteem. They are constantly picking to feel better about themselves and their own shortcomings. We all know people like this; they are usually the bullies. Someone who is confident and self-loving will never have to raise his or her voice, let alone a fist. Knowing this makes it easier to forgive someone who have wronged us and helps us to understand why a person acts in such a negative way. I personally don't just walk away from such negativity, I run! I don't see the need to be around it, and I also don't want to feed it. Sometimes when there is tension or anger in your surroundings, it is best to walk away from the situation and fill your lungs and heart with fresh, clean air without tension.

Hopefully, whatever caused the bad vibes will neutralize, and you can wish well on the place. I believe in karma, and what you wish for others will always come back to you tenfold. I try to remind myself of this every time I am in a peculiar situation and pray for a good outcome. Anger and distress harden our hearts and fills us with grief that will spill over into any setting, so we need to fill our hearts with a forgiving nature and know that the more we forgive, the more we will be forgiven.

ONE WEEK LEFT

Most of us will never know when we will take our last breath in this lifetime until we take it, be we do know for a fact that at any second it could be our last. Death does not know anything about timing: it can take babies, teenagers, parents, friends, or great-grandparents. We know that anyone can choke on the chicken, get hit by a car, have a heart attack, or fall asleep and never wake up. No matter how we pass on to the next stage, we are sure that it will happen. We should make the best of everyday now.

We have many teachers in life on how to live but not many on how to die. Instead, we fear death. Death is not something to be feared; death is just another stage of our lives. Our physical bodies don't live on, but our spirits do. If we make a loving impression or difference in lives here on earth, then we will be remembered as good, and we will live on through our loved ones.

We get caught up in the worries and stress of life. We sometimes must struggle with the bills and sometimes even with worldly riches. We forget that we are not going to be able to take those riches with us when our bodies die, and thankfully we won't be able to take the bills either. The only thing we have to take is our spirits, or our souls; the rest stays here after we are gone. Why do we worry so much about competing with each other over who has more worldly materials when we really should compete for who can yield more laughs and smiles every day? Wouldn't that be a nice contest?

Imagine that you are told by your doctor that you have one week to live. Who would you call? What would you say? Knowing every time you see a person might be the last time you will see them here on this earth, will you tell them what you think of them? Will you say you love them? Why was it also so hard to say "I love you?" What would be the worst that could happen? That they may not say it back? Who cares? You don't love conditionally, expecting it back. You love unconditionally because love is life. Love is what makes us feel good and alive. Why do we waste time and energy on stuff that doesn't even matter? For example, I spent hours fixing up my bathroom wall from a leak. I could not wait to get home to get more of the wall fixed. I was in such a hurry to just get it done that I forgot to call my Mom to say goodnight. That bathroom wall will never say goodnight to me, give me a hug, or tell me that it loves me (if it does, I will definitely run out of my house and never return.) However, my mom did do all those things!

We need to remember that our time here on earth is limited, and we need to show our love, listen to everyone, step on the grass, and enjoy the rain. It is all going to be here after us, so make it playful because there will never be such a thing as too much fun. We seem to appreciate life more when we are closer to death, so we should act as if we only had a week left. In this way, life will become more precious. Life is like anything else; when we have it in abundance, we waste more of it. When we know we have only a limited supply, then we appreciate it more. Let's get out there and have some fun. Make a difference in people's lives, even if it is just by smiling, laughing, or saying a kind word to a stranger. The passion for life that we put out there will pass on to all, and it will spread like warm butter.

In the final moments with my mom and my brother Jack, their strength shone like a beacon of light in the midst of darkness. It was as if they had this unwavering courage that radiated from them, casting away any traces of fear. Despite the challenges they faced, they carried themselves with a grace that amazed us all. I remember their smiles, those gentle expressions that seemed to reassure us that everything would be okay. It was as if they held a secret, a deep knowing that they were about to embark on a new journey, reuniting with the loved ones who had gone before them. Their ability to live those last days with such strength not only comforted them, but it became the strength for the rest of us, a reminder that love and connection transcend the boundaries of life and death.

CHAPTER THREE: COMMON GROUND

WORK

The one thing that most of us have in common is that we all must work for a living. We spend a considerable amount of time at work and really need to remember not to let work take over our lives. We need to balance work and home life; this gets even more important as we get older. I've seen so many people devote their entire lives to their careers only to die within weeks of their retirement. The reason for that scenario could be that they put all their effort into work and forgot how to live. The only thing they focused on was their job, and they forgot how to enjoy the wonderful day without stress.

I admit that I love all the challenges at work. I even love the pressure of the day at work. I sometimes need to remind myself that work doesn't make my life important; I make work important. We sometimes think that what we do for a living or how much power we have at work decides how important we are, but this is the furthest thing from the truth. I was out to dinner the other night and was waiting for my Shirley Temple to come out when I overheard the manager screaming at my waiter that she doesn't care what the customer wanted and that she was in charge, not the customer. I thought, "Wow! Doesn't she know that the customers are the ones making it possible to have the work? All I was asking for was an extra cherry in my drink!"

We sometimes need to be reminded that it really is how we do our work and how we treat others that is important. If we move up the ladder in the jobs we are in, we need to remember that for every step up, we will need to come back down; it's the power of gravity. One of the mistakes co-workers sometimes make is thinking of others as competition, this is a mistake.

Embracing collaboration over competition offers huge benefits for both our spiritual well-being and our pursuit of success. When we choose to work together, we tap into shared knowledge, diverse perspectives, and collective wisdom. This fosters an environment of mutual support and growth, aligning with the principles of empathy, kindness, and understanding that are often central to spiritual development.

In a collaborative setting, individuals complement each other's strengths and compensate for weaknesses, creating a harmonious synergy that fuels innovation and progress. The act of cooperating itself can be deeply fulfilling, as it nurtures a sense of belonging and connection, fulfilling our need for community and social interaction. Through collaboration, we break down the barriers that isolate us and instead cultivate a sense of unity and shared purpose.

From a success standpoint, working together provides a solid foundation for achievement that transcends the limitations of competition. Rather than exhausting resources and energy in cut throat rivalries, collaboration enables the pooling of resources, skills, and knowledge, enhancing efficiency and effectiveness. This approach encourages an abundance mindset, as individuals recognize that success isn't a finite resource, but rather a collective achievement that can be shared and celebrated.

Moreover, collaboration tends to foster a positive and supportive atmosphere, nurturing the growth of individuals and teams. The open exchange of ideas encourages learning, adaptability, and continuous improvement, qualities essential for sustained success in our rapidly evolving world. Collaborators are also more likely to remain motivated and engaged, as the shared goals and mutual support bolster resilience in the face of challenges.

Ultimately, by choosing collaboration over competition, we align ourselves with higher spiritual values while also optimizing our chances for success. This path allows us to evolve as individuals, contribute positively to the collective whole, and create a legacy built on unity, empathy, and shared accomplishment.

The bottom line is to do your job the best you can and be grateful that you are able to work. Always remember that work is an important part of our lives, and we should take pride in it, but we need to take pride in our rest, too. We are not machines, and when we take time to relax, we will end up doing a better, more efficient job in the long run. We can't make our jobs and careers our only priority because we forget to slow down and enjoy the here and now when we do that. I had a boss once tell me that if I wanted to earn more money in the company, I should leave my partner (he was not liked by him because I rushed home in the evenings to be with him and I still do) and stay late with the other managers because the best business plans happened over a few drinks. Those few words told me everything I needed to know about the businesspeople to whom I was helping to build a successful company.

I think of work as a relationship. If you try to better each other and grow, you will prosper. If you treat each other with respect, that loyalty will inevitably grow. If you work smart and hard and have good work ethics, then you should be compensated for your efforts. If you have a lousy paying job or a job where you do not agree with the morals of the administration, then you should look inside of yourself honestly and evaluate why you are in such a situation. You should also decide to make the small changes in your daily life that are needed, but whatever you do, please don't blame everyone else. There will always be people who will not be helpful in trying to see you succeed, but don't let that discourage you because they are nervous about their own shortcomings. Watch and learn from the people who are happy to be at work, the people who are successful because they know how to do it. Keep going, and nothing will be able to stop you.

People are judged by the company they keep, and I have always felt that a company should be judged by how they treat employees. If everyone is rewarded for the quality of work that is done, then the company will be successful. If the company leaders are honest and caring, then the rest of the company will follow suit. If the company leaders are shallow and cheat, then why wouldn't those traits trickle down to everyone else? This is true with every aspect of life. We lead by example not by words alone. We all need to remember that we are a team and that a team will win when its members work together and help each other along the way. Competition is healthy and beneficial, but only when the individuals help others to win, too.

IT'S NOT WHAT YOU HAVE BUT WHAT YOU ARE

I know a guy who made twenty-five thousand dollars a year and retired at sixty because he lived comfortably, budgeted his money well, and truly valued the company of others, not the luxuries bought with money. I went to many of his picnics where everyone brought their own potluck dish to share, and he would make it exciting for everyone to see how little it would cost to throw such a shindig. I know another guy who was the CEO of a major corporation, worked until he was sixty-seven years old, and retired financially broke because he was so used to the luxuries of corporate life and would throw parties costing thousands of dollars. After his retirement, not one of those guests would show up to his picnics because they only attended country club parties. I would much rather walk into the first guy's shoes and have the riches of love.

Someone once told me that "money is the root of all evil," and I couldn't help myself from laughing out loud. When I finally stopped laughing, I simply said, "Money in the hands of a good-natured person will only do good. Money does not have the power to do evil, it is us who have that power. My mom was surrounded by grandkids, her kids, family, and friends all the time in her home. She was blessed to have so much love surrounding her because she truly loved everyone. That is what makes life worthwhile and important, not the fancy cars, houses, or luxury curtains. I remember visiting my mom and finding my first book that I wrote for my parents when I was ten years old. I was shocked at what I read. The very first line of the book reminded me of what I always knew. Twenty-five years later, I was in the middle of writing a book about the very same subject. It read, "God is Love." If I knew that at ten years old and believed it enough to actually write about it at that age, then I figure being rich is really about being yourself and surrounding yourself with love. You know, when we talk about God being love, it's like we're saying that love is at the core of everything divine. It's not just about a feeling we have for someone special, but this incredible force that connects all of us. It's like the warm hug of the universe, reminding us that kindness, compassion, and understanding are all part of something bigger. So, when we try to live with love in our hearts, we're actually getting a glimpse of something truly divine.

When I am doing the sales end of my business, I have always been completely honest with every client, and I will never change that because I trust in others. I know for a fact that when you are completely straightforward and believe in what you are doing, then the work will always be there. I have never been fearful of losing clients because I know that every time I save money for clients or let them know that they do not need my services at this time, they will spread the word about how honest my company and its representatives are. I truly believe that if you trust in your heart, you will not only have an abundance of luck and love, but you will also be golden with a stable career, even in tough economic times.

"United we stand, divided we fall." Isn't that the truth in everything in life? Whether we are trying to build a stable career, a happy family, a strong neighborhood, or a government, we must try to remember those six famous words. Let's take those words for what they are and remember that we are all connected on some level. I believe that we are all connected through love. It doesn't matter what we do for a living, what we have financially, what religious beliefs that we may or may not have, or even what political stands we take. We must remember to take those words into work, home, church, school, or wherever we go and try to have patience for others' views. Thankfully, everyone is different. Imagine if we were all the same. What a boring existence we would have. Let's try to have less arguments and listen just a little bit more. If we do so, there will be fewer problems in this world.

Picture a heart, like yours or mine, that's shining with light. Imagine that this light is so bright and warm that it can never fade away. No matter how tough things get, this light keeps on shining, spreading its glow to everyone around. Just like a cozy campfire on a dark night, this light brings comfort and hope.

And you know what's really amazing? This light in our hearts is a lot like love and kindness. It's something we can share freely, and the more we give, the more it grows. Love isn't like a pie that gets smaller when you share it – it's more like a magic pie that keeps getting bigger and tastier!

Think about money and love as if they're good vibes that can spread from one person to another. There's this endless supply of good vibes out there, like stars in the sky. When we're kind to others or share what we have, it's like adding more stars to the sky. And guess what? Those stars multiply and light up the whole night.

So remember, just like a heart filled with light can never be dim, there's more than enough love and good vibes for everyone. And the coolest part is, when you spread love and kindness, it's like you're passing around a cheerful bug – a good kind of bug that makes people smile and want to be kind too. So, let's keep shining our heart lights and sharing those good vibes, because together, we can make the world a brighter and happier place! It will be so contagious that all negativity, sorrow, and hate will drown in the sea of love forever.

Let me tell this story to explain what I mean:

In the heart of a busy city, there lived a man named John who had fallen on hard times. Once a successful businessman, he had lost his job and his home in a series of unfortunate events. Now, he found himself homeless, wandering the crowded streets with little more than the clothes on his back and a heart heavy with despair.

One chilly evening, as John sat on a park bench, hunger gnawing at his stomach, a kind stranger approached him. This stranger, named Sarah, offered John a warm meal and a friendly smile. Grateful and touched by her generosity, John accepted the food and struck up a conversation with Sarah. They talked for hours, and in that time, John learned that Sarah was part of a local charity organization that helped homeless individuals.

Moved by Sarah's compassion and inspired by her dedication to helping those less fortunate, John asked if there was any way he could repay her kindness. Sarah simply replied, "Help someone else when you can, and that will be repayment enough."

With newfound hope and a sense of purpose, John decided to volunteer at the very shelter that Sarah worked for. He spent his days helping to prepare meals, distribute warm clothing, and provide companionship to others who had fallen on hard times, just like him. As he listened to their stories and shared his own experiences, he realized that he had something valuable to offer beyond material possessions—a listening ear, empathy, and a willingness to lend a helping hand.

Word of John's dedication and compassion soon spread throughout the shelter, and he became known as a beacon of hope for those who felt lost and forgotten. Over time, he reconnected with old friends and used his network to help some of his fellow shelter residents find employment and housing opportunities.

As John continued to give of himself to others, he noticed something remarkable happening. Strangers began offering him assistance, too. Some provided him with temporary shelter during harsh weather, while others offered him job leads. It seemed as though the universe was repaying his kindness.

One day, Sarah approached John with exciting news. She had managed to secure him a job interview, thanks to a connection she had made during her work with the charity. John aced the interview and landed a new job, slowly but surely regaining his footing in life.

John's story serves as a powerful reminder that it's not what you have that matters most, but what you give to help others. He learned that when you extend kindness and compassion to those in need, it has a way of coming back to you, often when you least expect it. John's journey from despair to hope, from receiving help to giving it freely, showed him that the true richness of life lies in the bonds we form and the good we do for others.

TRUST

One of the best feelings in the world is when we have trust in ourselves and others. The easiest way to trust others is by trusting yourself. Be honest with yourself and listen to your instincts or inner voice. Know that it is not always about who is right or wrong; sometimes it is better to just be happy and take a step back to see the situation from another point of view. Express yourself and your thoughts the way you want, knowing that you are unique and that no one will ever be the same as you. That is what makes you special. I know that I laugh funny, but what a blessing it is to be able to laugh and listen to everyone else's laughter. Trust in that laughter; it comes from happiness.

Because God is love, that makes Satan or hell evil. In all religious beliefs God is forgiving, with unconditional love for all of us. God does not judge us or punish us for our mistakes; we punish ourselves and each other through fear. Remember always that fear or lack of is the easiest way for others to take advantage or manipulate. No one is perfect and God knows that. We all must do the best we can and know that we can and should learn from our mistakes. Live and learn and stop condemning each other through fear, which creates our living hells here on earth. Get rid of all that fear, pity, and hate. The illusion of hell will then disappear, and trust will grow.

Trust is an amazing feeling; it's strong and blameless. We shouldn't blame each other for the small things that won't even affect our daily lives. We should not meddle in other's lives, and we should just plain and simple mind our own business. We should never pay back evil with evil. According to one of my favorite sayings, you should, "Turn your hate into love and you shall be loved." When we believe in trust or truth, we can never be condemned for enjoying the evil. When someone lies or cheats us, it is an ugly feeling; a feeling of sadness washes over us. We all have been hurt by someone's distrust, but we need to remember that if we try to close down our hearts so that we won't be hurt again, we are really only hurting ourselves. Forgive whoever cheated you and you will become much stronger for it. Just remember that once is a mistake and twice is a habit. At that point, you shouldn't only walk away from that person, but run!

As we journey through life, one of the most essential qualities we can develop is the ability to trust ourselves and others. Our instincts, those gut feelings that guide us, play a vital role in making the right choices. This chapter explores how we can embrace these instincts to navigate our path with responsibility, honesty, gratitude, and a compassionate desire to help others.

Imagine you're standing at a crossroads, unsure of which path to take. In times like these, your instincts act as your inner compass. They're like a friend who knows you well and whispers advice when you need it most. Learning to trust these feelings takes practice. Begin by paying attention to how you react to different situations. Your body might tense up in discomfort or light up with excitement. These physical cues are your instincts communicating with you. Trusting yourself means acknowledging these feelings and allowing them to guide you, even if they don't always seem logical at first.

Trusting others can be a delicate dance. Just as you rely on your instincts, understanding others' intentions requires careful observation. Start by giving people the benefit of the doubt, but remain cautious until actions consistently align with words. Trust isn't built overnight; it grows over time through shared experiences and consistent reliability. Remember, trusting others doesn't mean ignoring your instincts. It means using them to assess who's worth opening up to.

A life rooted in trust is built on the sturdy foundation of responsibility and honesty. When you make a promise or commit to something, follow through. This not only demonstrates your reliability to others but also to yourself. Honesty, on the other hand, is like clear water running through your actions. Be truthful with yourself and others, even when the truth is difficult. It might feel uncomfortable, but it prevents unnecessary complications down the road.

Living with gratitude is like planting seeds of positivity that bloom into a vibrant garden. As you navigate life's twists and turns, take a moment to reflect on the good things. Whether it's a sunny day, a kind word from a friend, or the opportunity to learn something new, practicing gratitude enhances your overall outlook. When you cultivate gratitude, you're also more likely to treat others with kindness and respect, nurturing a cycle of positivity.

One of the most fulfilling aspects of life is extending a helping hand to others. As you develop trust in yourself and the world around you, remember to lift others up. Whether it's a small act of kindness or a larger endeavor, offering assistance not only benefits those you help but also strengthens your own character. Helping others fosters a sense of interconnectedness and reminds us that we're all part of a larger plan and we all really are here for a reason. I truly believe that we are born with certain things that we must accomplish within our lifetime. I think we know what it is but with all the noise in life we get distracted and those things become forgotten, but that doesn't mean we shouldn't search for them and work toward accomplishing good along the way.

In conclusion, the journey of trusting yourself and others is a dance of intuition, responsibility, honesty, gratitude, and compassion. Just like any skill, it takes time to master. So, as you continue to navigate through life, listen to your instincts, trust your inner compass, and extend trust to those who prove worthy. Embrace your role in creating a more harmonious world, where gratitude and the desire to help others shine brightly along your path.

LIGHTEN UP

Stress, I feel it when my shoulders start to tense up and it feels like I'm wearing shoes that are a size too small. We all get stressed and frustrated at times, and that is okay, but we need to remember to just lighten up. We are bombarded by horrible things on the news almost every day, but we need to realize that the news is full of the unusual, not the usual. If it were the usual, then it would not have made it into the news. We sometimes worry about all the wrong things: the end of the world, what others think of us or expect of us, or what we expect of others.

Surround yourself with happy people and remember that being happy is not just a feeling or an emotion; it is second nature. We have the ability to decide whether we are happy or sad, fulfilled or desperate, and even wealthy or poor. We need to just lighten up and be ourselves. We need to be grateful for all the beauty that surrounds us and be part of it by really taking the time to enjoy it. When we learn to manage our time and do everything that we do in moderation and not go overboard on anything, then we will have spare time to see what we have been looking for. The problem is that we are always looking for everything. Stop looking so hard and let your second nature take over. If we are constantly looking for happiness, it may pass us by when we have had it all along. If we are looking for love, it's probably within sight already; we just have to reach out and give a loving hug. We need to take risks to gain rewards. That is why they are called rewards.

You know, it's funny how we've come to a point where we often reward just showing up or putting in some effort, even if it's just average. Don't get me wrong, hard work and dedication are definitely important, but sometimes it feels like we're handing out trophies for participation rather than actual achievement. Trophies were originally meant to celebrate winners, those who excelled and stood out from the rest. And that's the thing – rewards like trophies should be reserved for those who truly earn them through their exceptional performance.

Losing or facing setbacks, whether in sports, work, or life in general, shouldn't be seen as a negative thing. It's all about perspective. Losing can be a stepping stone to growth and improvement. It's through those challenges and failures that we learn, adapt, and become better versions of ourselves. In fact, some of the most valuable life lessons come from not always winning, but from how we handle defeat and what we do with that experience.

This philosophy isn't just for kids – it applies to adults as well. We all face challenges and disappointments, and the mindset we adopt makes a huge difference. If we focus on constant improvement and doing our absolute best, regardless of the outcome, we're setting ourselves up for success in the long run. It's like the law of attraction – if we put in the effort and truly believe in our ability to achieve greatness, it's more likely that we'll attract positive outcomes. So, instead of seeking rewards for mediocrity, let's embrace the journey of growth, aim for excellence, and let the real rewards come from the satisfaction of knowing we gave it our all.

It is important to set goals and work toward them because it gives us strength and courage to keep going to better ourselves. When we put outrageous goals on others, it will slow them down because they fear disappointing us. We must show by example and change the way we teach by the way we actually live.

Ah, my recent trip to Maine was an eye-opener, let me tell you. So, there I was, all set for a relaxing vacation, but guess what? I forgot my phone at home. Panic mode, right? I mean, how was I going to survive without it? It's practically an extension of my hand. But then it hit me – this was my chance to really disconnect and unwind.

At first, I admit, I was a bit uneasy. Work worries kept creeping in. What if someone needed something urgently? What if I missed out on important updates? But then, a realization struck me like a breath of fresh Maine air – I had earned this break. Those days were mine to do with as I pleased. So, I made a conscious decision to let go of work stress and focus on the present moment.

And you know what? It was like a weight lifted off my shoulders. Instead of staring at my phone, I was gazing at the stunning coastal views. I swapped emails for seashells and meetings for leisurely walks. I allowed myself to be silly, to laugh without restraint, and to embrace the joy of slowing down. It's incredible how taking a step back from the hustle and bustle can do wonders for your mental and physical health.

I realized that I'd been caught up in the fast lane for way too long, neglecting the simple pleasures of life. Maine taught me that being fully present and letting go of unnecessary worries is a form of self-care. It's a reminder that we need to find that balance between work and play, seriousness, and silliness. So, if you ask me, my unplugged vacation in Maine was a lesson well learned – sometimes, it's the moments we're not capturing on our phones that truly capture our hearts. Another little fact is all my published books were finished on the same balcony in Ogunquit, Maine.

CHAPTER FOUR: LIFE LESSONS

BE CAREFUL OF THE WOLF IN SHEEP'S CLOTHING

We all want to be happy and live a peaceful life but every once in a while, the devil will come along disguised as a sheep. The sheep appears to be gentle, kind, and loving but in time, you find your good nature has been compromised. After a while, you find the sheep has been clawing away at your good nature while all along trying his best to destroy you, not knowing that love is much more powerful than anger, hate, or deception. The devil is just a lonely, sad, and angry being who is only happy when others are brought down to his level. I believe most people attempt to be good, but we sometimes take rockier paths in life and become lost. We tend to panic when we feel lost because we are not in control of where we are going and don't want to end up somewhere unknown to us. It is at that point where we must choose the path we want to take, knowing we make our own decisions in life and must live with the results. We must realize it is foolish to blame the outcome on others.

When we pretend to be something we are not, we are only deluding ourselves. When we are deceived by wolves in sheep's clothing we become stronger knowing the devil didn't have any power over us because, we were filled with the natural light of Love that blinded the wolf's angry vision. Do not let the wolf's addiction slow you down on your happy trail in life; keep the peaceful spirit and loving thoughts in your heart and you will never have to fear the mean devil. Life is about how we handle challenges, through what we learn from those challenges and how we treat others in our daily lives. Always try to help others and you will be surrounded by Love, but when you come across an angry devil who tries to hurt you, remember not to stoop down to his level. Surround yourself with family and friends who love and care for you unconditionally.

We all have been deceived and feel used at times by people with mean spirited motives. We may even feel like getting even or settling the score but let me tell you from my own experience, it is never worth it! We should never attempt to stoop to the mean-spirited persons level in order to feel a few moments of gratification because we will have to live with our actions. I have learned at an early age, the only person who is always going to be there for me always is me, but I want to able to lie my head down on my pillow at night knowing I did well that day. We learn a lot about ourselves and others when we are under pressure, filled with stress, and in heated situations. We learn we may have a temper, or we may get scared. We may even become defensive, or we can overcome that stress from the strength we have from within our inner faith and the love we have for others.

Let me tell you this little story to help explain trying to live with compassion and seeing others ways and motives before passing judgement:

In a serene village nestled between rolling hills, lived a kind-hearted shepherd named Lucas. Lucas was known far and wide for his compassion, humility, and his ability to understand and forgive. His flock of sheep grazed peacefully under his watchful eye, and he treated each of them with utmost care and love.

One crisp morning, Lucas noticed a lone wolf lurking at the edge of his pastures. Instead of reacting with fear or anger, Lucas approached the wolf cautiously, trying to understand its plight. He saw that the wolf was limping, its eyes filled with pain and hunger.

Lucas realized that the wolf's actions were driven by desperation rather than malice.

Filled with empathy, Lucas brought the injured wolf into his small cottage. He tended to its wounds, fed it, and offered a warm place by the fire. The wolf, initially wary, gradually began to trust Lucas. Over time, they shared stories and experiences, and the wolf learned about Lucas's way of life.

As the days turned into weeks, the wolf's demeanor started to change. It began to see the world through Lucas's eyes, understanding the value of compassion, gratitude, and forgiveness. The wolf realized how its past actions had caused harm and fear among the villagers and Lucas's flock. It felt a deep remorse and understood the importance of changing its ways.

One day, when the wolf had fully recovered, it asked Lucas for his forgiveness. Lucas smiled kindly and said, "Forgiveness is a gift we give not only to others but also to ourselves. By forgiving, we release the burden of anger and resentment, allowing room for understanding and healing." The wolf was deeply moved by Lucas's words and vowed to mend its ways.

With Lucas's guidance, the wolf started to help protect the flock instead of preying on it. It became a loyal guardian, using its strength to fend off other predators and keep the sheep safe. The villagers were initially hesitant, but Lucas vouched for the wolf's transformation, and slowly, trust began to build.

Over time, the wolf's selfless actions spoke louder than its past, and the villagers started to see the goodness within it. They realized that just as Lucas had shown forgiveness, they too should extend it to the reformed wolf. The village transformed into a place of understanding and unity, where both humans and animals co-existed peacefully.

Lucas's unwavering compassion and forgiveness had not only saved a wolf but had also mended the fabric of the village community. His ability to see beyond the surface and his willingness to offer a second chance taught everyone the power of empathy, patience, and putting oneself in another's shoes.

And so, the village's story spread, reminding all who heard it that while it's easy to judge from appearances, true change and healing come from understanding, gratitude, and the willingness to forgive. Just like Lucas, they strived to be forgiving shepherds, guiding others towards a path of transformation and unity.

LAUGHING

Laughter is the purest form of energy known to all humankind. Laughter is very contagious. Studies have shown that people who laugh every day live healthier and happier lives. Laughter is an unconscious vocalization; when we laugh, it comes from our inner self, without our control. Whenever we subconsciously do something, it becomes second nature. Studies from all over the world agree on two major facts; laughter can eliminate physical pain and it helps stabilize our blood pressure.

Laughter is like a magical medicine that eases stress and brings joy. When we laugh, our worries seem to lighten, and the weight of stress melts away. It's like a little burst of happiness that spreads warmth through our hearts. Science shows that laughter releases feel-good chemicals in our brains, making us feel happier and more relaxed. So, when life feels heavy, sharing a good laugh can be a wonderful way to find relief and let happiness shine through.

When I am having a challenging day, I open a comic book and read it for a few moments or watch a funny movie to have a few laughs and just get away from the challenges of that moment. One of the best ways to get back into a good mood is to take a walk with nature, whether it is in the park, a bike ride through the city, or a stroll on the beach. Nature is the best way for us to relax and regain our happy state of mind. When we were babies, we would cry if we wanted a bottle or wanted to be held, because we didn't have any other way to communicate, and crying is natural and healthy like laughter.

There are thousands of languages and cultures in this great world of ours and the universal communicator we all know is laughter; this should be proof enough for us that we need to laugh more often. Laughter makes us look younger, feel younger, and healthier. It is so much easier to go up to a stranger and strike up a conversation with that person when we see the person laughing, because we know he or she is happy. Laughter is an energy changer and good for us all. Here is another small story about how laughter saved a community:

In a diverse village nestled in the heart of a lush valley, people from various backgrounds and cultures lived together harmoniously. However, a challenge arose one day when the village well, the main water source, broke down, leaving the villagers in distress. The community had always thrived on communication, but with different languages spoken, finding a solution became difficult.

As tensions rose, a wise elder named Amira stepped forward. Amira was known for her ability to bridge gaps between people using her infectious laughter. She believed that laughter could transcend language barriers and unite hearts. Gathering everyone in the village square, she began to share a story, using gestures and expressions that made people chuckle.

Curious, people gathered, their attention piqued by Amira's animated storytelling. Although they couldn't understand the words, her expressive face and jovial tone elicited laughter from the crowd. Soon, a ripple of giggles spread throughout the assembly, and people from different language backgrounds found themselves laughing together.

Inspired by Amira's lighthearted approach, a young girl named Sofia started mimicking animals and using exaggerated motions, causing more laughter. The laughter became a bridge between the villagers, connecting them in a way words couldn't. With newfound unity, they collectively brainstormed ideas to fix the well.

Despite the language barriers, the villagers worked as a team, combining their strengths and problem-solving skills. Laughter continued to play a role, helping to break down the walls of miscommunication. Days passed, and the villagers managed to repair the well, their efforts bolstered by their shared laughter and determination.

The village thrived once again, and the incident became a cherished memory. From that day on, laughter was celebrated as a universal language within the community. People would often gather in the square, sharing jokes and funny stories, creating a sense of togetherness that transcended language differences. The power of laughter had saved the day and had woven an unbreakable bond among the diverse inhabitants of the village, proving that a hearty laugh can communicate where words fail.

TOUGH LOVE

What is tough love and what does it mean to you? I know for me it is a difficult subject but one we all may encounter in our lives, because we don't live in a perfect world. I have a close friend who is a drug addict and has been fighting the habit for many years. I have tried to be there for this person and found it is a challenging roll to play because, when dealing with an addiction, you trust the drugs and not the person who is on the drugs. In my first book, Life in a Week; A Book About Being Really Happy, I tell a story about the mama bird who pushes the baby birds out of the nest. The baby bird starts to fall but she instinctively starts to fly! This is the proudest time of the mama bird's life and at the same time, it is the most difficult time. Tough love is what the mama bird inherently must do in order for the babies to live. Sometimes, it is what friends must do for friends to survive in this world.

If you have an addiction, it is important to find out what is bothering you enough to turn to the addiction as a temporary or long-term fix. It is important to find the solution to the situations in your life and fix the problem. Remember, it is the "lame wolf" devil who lures addicts away from their problems, not true friends. If everyone seems to have lost trust in your word due to lies you have told, only you can be honest with yourself, and trust will be regained as time goes on. The only person who you will be with your entire life is you; so, you'd better like yourself! Enjoy the day reminding yourself, as long as you do better today than you did yesterday, you are heading down a good path in life. Never be afraid to ask for help because there are many who will love to help you. Either they love you or they may too have even been in your same situation at one time or another.

It's fascinating how the perspective on addiction and alcoholism has evolved over the years. Modern medicine often views them as diseases, influenced by genetic, physiological, and neurological factors. This approach emphasizes the complex interplay of brain chemistry and the body's response to substances. However, there are those, like me, who believe that the root cause of addiction might go beyond the physiological realm.

My personal experience sheds light on this alternative perspective. For years, I struggled with excessive drinking, unable to break free from its grip. But then, something unexpected happened when I confronted my own inner struggles. At the age of 42, I acknowledged and embraced my own identity as a gay individual, dispelling years of self-imposed homophobia. Astonishingly, as I came to terms with my truth and faced it head-on, my addiction simply vanished. This experience led me to believe that deep-seated emotional issues can indeed play a pivotal role in addiction.

This belief highlights the power of introspection and self-awareness. Our thoughts and emotions shape our realities more than we realize. When we're honest with ourselves and face our inner demons, we can create profound shifts in our lives. This concept isn't limited to addiction; it extends to various aspects of our existence. Trusting our instincts and using our imagination to mold the life we desire can be remarkably transformative.

While the debate between the disease model and the psychological approach continues, there's something to be said for the notion that addressing the emotional underpinnings of addiction can yield surprising results. By understanding the factors that lead us down such paths and by fostering genuine honesty within ourselves, we might indeed uncover a more comprehensive way to heal and recover. After all, our personal truths, when acknowledged and embraced, hold the potential to reshape the course of our lives in powerful and unexpected ways. I can say this with complete certainty because I live it each day.

When we truly love someone, we will rejoice in his or her joy, successes, and happiness. So why not do the same for us: When someone we love has an addiction, we must remember to show this individual we have unconditional love for him or her. We must never tell this person what to do and must have patience when helping them to get out of the fog in which they surround themselves. We need to remind them you don't need to search for happiness, because it is already in all of us. Tough love means, we might have to step back and pray that our loved one will learn from his mistakes and move forward as a stronger person.

It's crucial to prioritize our own well-being when dealing with tough love and helping others. This story illustrates that point:

In a small town, lived a young man named Alex. Alex had fallen deep into the clutches of addiction, and his parents, Mary and John, were desperate to help him break free. They tried everything they could think of to support him in getting clean. They enrolled him in rehab programs, attended therapy sessions as a family, and even reached out to support groups.

However, despite their best efforts, Alex seemed resistant to change. He would show glimpses of progress, only to relapse again and again. Mary and John were torn between their love for their son and their growing exhaustion from the emotional roller coaster of his addiction. They had invested so much time, energy, and hope into his recovery, yet it seemed like a never-ending challenge.

Realizing that their own well-being was at stake, Mary and John sought guidance from a counselor. The counselor emphasized the importance of setting boundaries and focusing on their own mental health. She explained that while their intentions were noble, they couldn't force Alex to change until he was ready.

With this newfound insight, Mary and John started attending support groups for families dealing with addiction. They found solace in connecting with others who were going through similar struggles. Slowly, they began to recenter their focus on their own lives and well-being. They pursued hobbies they had set aside and rekindled friendships they had neglected.

Over the next two years, Alex continued to battle his addiction, facing setbacks and relapses. But as Mary and John continued to prioritize their own emotional health, something shifted within them. They learned that they couldn't control their son's choices, but they could control how they responded to the situation.

One day, after a particularly tough relapse, Alex approached his parents with strong determination. He expressed his desire to finally overcome his addiction and acknowledged the toll it had taken on his family. Mary and John, now armed with their own emotional resilience, embraced him with love and support.

Alex's journey to recovery wasn't without its challenges, but with his parents in a healthier mindset, they were better equipped to provide the unwavering support he needed. It was a long and challenging road, but their experience highlighted the importance of putting one's own well-being first when helping others navigate through their struggles. That is tough love at its finest, do not ever feel guilty for stepping back or using tough love to help, it is much more powerful than we may know.

WHERE WE ARE

We create our tomorrows by our actions today. Every action creates a reaction; it is that simple! We really do create our own destiny and I do not believe in chance or coincidence. This is true with everything in life whether we are trying to better our home life, work situations, school grades, or social activities. If you want to be loved, show love; if you want to be rich, work smarter; if you want to have closer friendships, be friendlier and show you really care.

We are only on this earth for a little while; so we really need to make the best of our limited time. I often wonder, how ready I am to enter into the next life? If today is my last day and tomorrow never comes, who will remember me, who will miss me? More importantly, whom have I helped to have a happier life? Is it true, when one is out of sight, one is quickly out of mind? What helps me enjoy life every day may seem cold or even gloomy, but it helps remind me our time is limited, so we really should make the most of it. In the morning, I consider for a moment, I may not live until the evening. By living this way, death will never take me by surprise, and I will never have to move onto the next stage with unfinished business left here on earth. These thoughts remind me never to go to bed having argued with a loved one.

Death is a fact of life that is a certainty and when we face that fact, we will live a much happier life. Each night as you lay your head on your pillow, think about the day that has just past you by. You can smile and know you did the best you could and can be satisfied by the events of the day. When you have major problems, don't try to tackle all of them in one day. Just chip away a little piece at a time. Trust me when I say, "It doesn't even matter, just be happy."

Sometimes, we are in places in life where we think, "the grass is greener on the other side of the fence." I often wonder what people are thinking, I can sit on a bench and watch people walk by and wonder by the expressions on their faces what they are thinking and where they are in the moment. I wonder if they know how lucky they are to be in such a great setting, with their friends and family or even just as a little getaway for an instant. Watching other people for a while, I realized I too, have it good and I am in a great place.

You know, it's quite remarkable how we often overlook the simple fact that every day we wake up is a gift in itself. It's like we get caught up in the rush of life and forget to truly appreciate the present moment. I remember a time when I began to realize just how fortunate I am to have each day at hand. It was a moment of re-flection, a realization that life is fleeting, and that the time we have is limited. Accepting the inevitability of death might seem morbid, but it actually became a source of wisdom for me. Embracing life each moment pushed me to fully experience each moment, to savor the beauty of the sunrise, the warmth of a smile, the laughter of loved ones, and the small joys that make up our days. It's a mindset that reminds me not to take anything for granted, and to live with gratitude and intention, cherishing every single day as the precious opportunity it truly is.

NEW DAY BRINGS A NEW BEGINNING

Here we are again with a perfect day to start fresh! Today is the first day of the rest of your life and the beginning of yet another great day of learning, growing, and Loving. Every year, I ask my family and friends "what is your new years resolution?" I get the same five or six responses. The most popular ones are; to spend more time with the family, lose weight and get more fit, quit smoking, quit drinking, get rid of debt, and to be more organized. Then I hear the random ones such as helping others more often, start volunteering, and learn something new. All are perfect resolutions and I am glad to see that. We all put the effort into bettering ourselves and the world around us, but we will be discouraged if we don't live up to the resolutions we made. In the long run, we will ultimately forget we made them.

New Year's resolutions often don't work as well as real, lasting change from within because they tend to be superficial and short-lived. Here's a simple explanation:

Lack of Depth: New Year's resolutions are typically vague and focused on the surface. For example, someone might resolve to "lose weight" or "exercise more." These goals lack the depth and specificity needed for real change.

External Pressure: Resolutions are often made because it's a tradition or because others are doing it. It's like a social pressure.

Real change, on the other hand, comes from a personal desire and commitment.

Quick Fix Mentality: Resolutions often stem from a desire for quick results. People expect immediate change, and when that doesn't happen, they get discouraged and give up. Real change is a gradual process that takes time and effort.

Lack of Planning: Resolutions often lack a concrete plan for how to achieve them. They're more like wishes than actionable goals. Real change requires a well-thought-out plan and consistent action.

No Emotional Connection: Resolutions are often made because they sound good, but there might not be a deep emotional connection to them. Real change comes when you're genuinely invested and motivated by your goals.

All-or-Nothing Thinking: People often have an all-or-nothing mentality with resolutions. If they slip up once, they feel like they've failed and abandon their goals. Real change allows for setbacks and learning from mistakes.

External Rewards: Resolutions are often tied to external rewards or validation (like looking good in a swimsuit). Real change comes from intrinsic motivation – doing something because it aligns with your values and makes you feel better about yourself.

In contrast, "change from within" means making changes because you genuinely want to, not because of external pressures or arbitrary dates like New Year's. It involves setting specific, meaningful goals, creating a plan, and being patient with yourself as you work toward those goals. Real change is driven by your inner motivations, values, and a commitment to becoming the best version of yourself.

Every day, we meet new people and find ourselves in new situations giving us an opportunity to learn something new and we may be surprised at the gems of wisdom that can affect us profoundly in our lives. We need to embrace fully; it is essential we acknowledge everyone is special in his or her own way. We tend to judge by appearances, status, and what we earn, this is a big mistake. If we make some new year's resolution to take an extra step in being a bit more compassionate, understanding, and kind to everyone who we come into contact with, we will have the potential to enrich our lives in such a big way! All relationships, whether brief or a life-long friend, can help us to open our eyes to new worlds of joy and happiness. We need to remember when we meet someone who we dislike or rubs us the wrong way, we still need to have that same compassion, while examining our own feelings carefully. Usually, the reason we may dislike someone who is different is because they compel us to question our own values and ideologies while, threatening to undermine our self-assurance.

We may sometimes dislike someone who is different because our initial reactions can be rooted in fear or discomfort stemming from unfamiliarity. Humans have a natural tendency to gravitate towards what's familiar and similar to their own experiences, which can lead to biases and prejudices against those who appear different. However, often, this dislike is based on misunderstanding rather than genuine reasons for conflict. The best way to bridge this gap and develop a more positive perspective is by being open to learning about their ways, cultures, and perspectives. By engaging in open-minded conversations, asking questions, and showing empathy, we can break down stereotypes, broaden our understanding, and realize that our differences often enrich our lives, fostering tolerance and harmony in diverse societies. Also, let me point out that listening more than talking is key. We tend to learn more when we listen than when we are constantly talking... just saying!

We need to treat others how we would like to be treated, not how we are treated. If we treat a negative action with a negative reaction, we will become that negative feeling. It is so important to remember that we attract more of what we feel, think about, and act on. Our thoughts become who we are in our daily lives. We need to start this new day with a positive and grateful attitude and spirit so we can work toward not only the best day of our lives but the rest of our lives as well. My point here is to start every day as a new beginning.

Small acts of kindness, like holding doors open, smiling, and appreciating the beauty in the world, can have a profound ripple effect. When we engage in these positive behaviors, we not only brighten someone else's day but also contribute to a more positive and harmonious environment. It's a reminder that our actions and attitudes can shape the world around us. By radiating positivity, we can inspire others to do the same, creating a cycle of kindness and appreciation that can make our communities and the world a better place for everyone.

The belief that we are all subconsciously connected as one and that our collective positivity can change the world is rooted in several philosophical and spiritual perspectives, such as interconnectedness and the ripple effect of our actions. Here's an explanation:

Interconnectedness: This perspective suggests that, at a fundamental level, everything and everyone in the universe is interconnected. It's like a vast web where every action, thought, or emotion of one person can have an impact on others and the world as a whole. This interconnectedness implies that we share a common thread of humanity and can influence each other in profound ways.

Collective Consciousness: Some belief systems propose the idea of a collective consciousness, a shared pool of thoughts, emotions, and energies that all humans tap into. When we collectively focus on positivity, kindness, and love, it is believed to have a positive influence on this collective consciousness.

Ripple Effect: Positive actions and attitudes can create a ripple effect. When one person acts positively, it can inspire others to do the same, creating a chain reaction of kindness and positivity. This can lead to a shift in the overall atmosphere and mindset of a community or even the world.

Self-Fulfilling Prophecy: The more we believe in our collective ability to make positive change, the more likely we are to take actions that align with that belief. When people collectively aim for positive change, they are more likely to work together, support one another, and channel their energies toward constructive goals.

Psychological Impact: Positivity is known to have psychological benefits. When people approach life with a positive mindset, they are more resilient, empathetic, and motivated to make a difference. These individual changes in mindset can collectively contribute to a more harmonious world.

In essence, the belief that we are all subconsciously connected and that our collective positivity can change the world is a hopeful and empowering perspective. It encourages us to take responsibility for our thoughts and actions, recognizing that our choices can influence not only our own lives but also the lives of others. By fostering a culture of positivity and kindness, we can indeed contribute to making the world a better place, one small step at a time each day!

HEADACHES

In the grand tapestry of existence, we are all threads woven together by energy. This energy is not just the force that powers our machines or lights up our cities; it is the subtle, invisible current that flows through every living being and connects us to the universe at large. It is the energy we exude that determines the energy we will attract, and in this chapter, we will explore how our thoughts, emotions, and actions shape the world around us.

Think of yourself as a beacon, radiating energy out into the world. This energy is not limited to your physical presence; it extends far beyond your body. It's the combination of your thoughts, emotions, and actions, all bundled together and projected into the universe.

Positive thoughts and emotions emit a vibrant, harmonious energy. When you're happy, content, and at peace with yourself, your energy resonates with the frequency of joy. This positivity acts like a magnet, drawing similar energies toward you. Have you ever noticed that when you're in a good mood, people around you tend to be more cheerful and receptive? It's not a coincidence; it's the energy you're emitting.

On the flip side, negative thoughts and emotions, such as anger, fear, or sadness, emit a disruptive energy. This energy can repel others or attract similar negativity. If you've ever been around someone who was visibly upset, you might have felt their negative energy and, consciously or not, tried to distance yourself from it.

The idea that like attracts like is a fundamental principle in the realm of energy. It's often referred to as the Law of Attraction.

This law suggests that the energy you emit is the energy you'll draw into your life. When you exude positivity, you naturally align with positive experiences, people, and opportunities. Conversely, dwelling in negativity tends to perpetuate a cycle of challenges and adversity.

Imagine two people, one radiating joy and gratitude, and the other steeped in bitterness and resentment. The first individual, with their positive energy, is likely to encounter situations and people that reinforce their happiness. The latter, however, might find themselves surrounded by similarly negative circumstances, seemingly trapped in a never-ending cycle of misery.

So, what does this mean for us in practical terms? It means that we have the power to shape our reality by consciously managing the energy we emit. When life throws challenges our way, as it inevitably will, we can choose how we respond. Instead of dwelling in negativity, we can acknowledge our feelings, learn from them, and then shift our focus toward solutions and gratitude.

Headaches, in a metaphorical sense, can be seen as the soul's way of telling us that something is amiss in our energy field. When we consistently emit negative energy, it can manifest as physical or emotional discomfort. It's a signal from our inner selves that it's time to change our thought patterns, attitudes, or actions. Our bodies have the power to heal themselves and headaches are not natural, just as sickness is not natural.

One of the most potent tools for shifting our energy toward positivity is laughter. Laughter is a universal language that transcends boundaries and connects us on a profound level. When we laugh, our energy becomes lighter, and our troubles seem to dissipate.

Laughter is not just a temporary escape; it's a healing force. It reduces stress, releases endorphins, and enhances our overall well-being. When we laugh, we open ourselves up to joy, and in doing so, we attract even more joy into our lives.

The energy we exude is the energy we will attract. By cultivating a positive mindset, nurturing our emotions, and choosing to radiate joy, we can shape our reality and draw in the abundance of positivity that surrounds us. And when life hands us challenges, we can heed the wisdom of our souls and transform our energy, knowing that laughter is one of the most potent cures for the ailments of the heart and soul.

Indeed, the idea that our bodies are vessels for our souls is a concept that has been pondered and cherished by various cultures and belief systems throughout human history. It touches on profound questions about the nature of existence, purpose, and the eternal aspects of the self. Let's explore this notion further:

Many philosophical and spiritual traditions suggest that our physical bodies are indeed temporary vessels for something greater - our souls. The body, in this view, is a finite and fragile container that houses the eternal and infinite essence of who we are. This perspective often invites contemplation about the quality of our existence, where the transient nature of the body contrasts with the enduring nature of the soul.

The idea that we are here to learn and grow is a theme that resonates with many belief systems. Whether through reincarnation, karma, or the pursuit of spiritual enlightenment, the concept of learning and evolving spiritually is a common thread.

In this view, life is seen as a journey of self-discovery and personal development. The experiences we encounter, both positive and negative, are opportunities for our souls to gain wisdom, compassion, and a deeper understanding of the universe and our place within it.

The belief that we are all here for a reason underscores the idea that everyone has a unique purpose or mission to fulfill during their time on Earth. This purpose can vary widely from person to person and may encompass everything from personal growth and self-realization to contributions to the greater good of humanity.

The search for one's purpose can be a lifelong quest, and many turn to religion, philosophy, or introspection to help uncover their mission in life. For some, this purpose may be connected to their talents, passions, or the impact they can make on the world. I truly believe that if we love unconditionally and help others without motives we are doing more than we even know to help the world and our own souls at the same time.

The idea that our souls live on even after our physical bodies cease to exist is a belief held by many spiritual traditions. It suggests that death is not the end but a transition, a passing from one state of existence to another.

This belief offers solace in times of grief and loss, as it implies that the essence of our loved ones endures in some form. It also raises profound questions about what lies beyond this life and the nature of the afterlife. As a volunteer for Hospice for many years I performed hundreds of death bed vigils and have personally seen spirits exiting their bodies, spirits hugging me on their way out with a beautiful feeling of peace and calmness surrounding me. I do not doubt that there is life after death and I do not fear moving onto the next stage of my soul's life, especially if I know that I have lived a life that has helped others.

In conclusion, the concept that our bodies are temporary vessels for our souls is a deeply philosophical and spiritual idea that has provided comfort and guidance to individuals throughout history. It encourages us to view life as a journey of learning, growth, and purpose, with the understanding that our souls continue their existence beyond the boundaries of our physical forms. Whether one subscribes to these beliefs or not, they offer a rich tapestry of perspectives on the nature of human existence and the quest for meaning.

KNOWING OURSELVES

As we journey deeper into the realm of self-discovery, I invite you to put on your metaphorical cape and unleash your inner superhero! Because guess what? You're extraordinary, and it's high time you acknowledged it.

Let's be honest, our thoughts can be like a monkey on an espresso binge—constantly hopping from one branch to another. Sometimes, they're swinging from the vines of unimportant things, or they're surfing the waves of wild fantasies. And oh boy, don't even get me started on the negative worries! But fear not, my friend, for we hold the power to transform this chaos into a symphony.

Our superhero journey begins with the realization that our quirks and uniqueness are our superpowers. It's time to break free from the mundane and embrace what makes you amazing. You see, when you recognize your true self-worth, you're like a sparkling diamond in a sea of rocks. You're not a carbon copy; you're the real deal, one-of-a-kind, and absolutely fabulous! So, let's wave good-bye to gossip and comparisons. They're like kryptonite for your self-esteem. Instead, sprinkle some self-love confetti over yourself every morning, and watch your self-worth skyrocket!

Now, onto our next mission: decoding the cryptic language of motives. Are your motives as pure as a freshly fallen snowflake, or are they as murky as a swamp? It's time to put on our detective hats and investigate.

Superheroes always act with noble intentions. They save the day not for fame or fortune, but because it's the right thing to do. Similarly, in our lives, we must ensure our motives are as pure as a clear mountain stream. When we act selflessly, the universe tends to conspire in our favor, making our life journey a whole lot smoother.

Every superhero has a heart full of goodness. Batman has his gadgets, Wonder Woman has her lasso, and you, my friend, have your heart—a powerful tool that can transform your life.

Cultivating a pure heart is like watering a magical garden within you. It involves planting seeds of compassion, kindness, and empathy. The more you nurture these qualities, the more they bloom, creating a fragrant garden of love in your soul. This garden will guide you in your quest for a decent life, where difficulties start to fade like distant memories.

Remember our secret weapon, the 'I Am' within? It's time to unleash its full potential! Getting to know your 'I Am' is like discovering a treasure chest filled with wisdom, purpose, and endless possibilities.

So, put on your explorer's hat and dive deep into your inner world. Ask questions, seek answers, and unlock the mysteries of your true self. As you do, you'll find that many problems start to dissolve like sugar in hot tea, leaving you with a sweet and harmonious life.

Remember this: You are the hero of your own story, and the power to change your life lies within you. Embrace your quirks, let your self-worth shine, act with pure motives, nurture a pure heart, and explore the depths of your 'I Am' within.

So, go ahead, my fellow superhero, and start your epic journey of self-discovery. Put on that cape of confidence, wield your heart's kindness, and let's face life's challenges head-on, knowing that with every step, you're becoming the superhero you were always meant to be.

In the grand comic book of life, every superhero has that defining moment, that epiphany when they realize their true potential. It's like the light bulb going off above their head, or in this case, above their superhero mask. And you, my friend, are about to have your superhero epiphany!

Our inner superhero, the wise and all-knowing part of us, often understands that we've crossed paths with a few mean-spirited folks along the way. Maybe they were the villains in our story, or maybe we played the role of the villain at times ourselves. It's a bit like a dramatic showdown between heroes and villains, with plot twists that would make even Hollywood jealous.

But here's the twist: dwelling in the past is like wearing a costume that no longer fits. It's uncomfortable, and it doesn't serve our superhero journey. Instead, our inner superhero knows that the power lies in the present moment. By focusing on the now, we can rewrite our story and change everything for the better.

As we take this empowering step forward, something truly magical happens. Those mean-spirited people, the villains of our past, start to fade away into the background like characters in a forgotten dream. Their power over us dissipates, making room for better relationships and incredible opportunities. It's like they vanish into thin air, leaving us free to soar to new heights.

But here's the golden nugget of wisdom: honesty is the trusty sidekick of our inner superhero. To move forward, we must be brutally honest with ourselves and learn from our mistakes. Every stumble, every misstep, every moment of deception becomes a valuable lesson in the superhero's handbook. And with each lesson learned, we become stronger, wiser, and more resilient.

So, my fellow superhero, let's leave the past behind, focus on the now, and let our inner truth guide us toward a brighter, more authentic future. As we do, we'll watch those mean-spirited characters dissolve into the mist, and in their place, we'll find the fertile ground for better relationships, boundless opportunities, and the heroic journey of a lifetime.

CHAPTER FIVE: SPIRITUALITY

RECOGNIZE FAULTS AND LET GO

In the heart of a quaint little town, nestled among narrow streets and centuries-old buildings, stood a magnificent church in Ecuador. It was a grand testament to the craftsmanship of a past era, its walls bearing the weight of history and devotion. People from all walks of life would gather there, seeking solace, inspiration, or simply a moment of quiet reflection.

One hot and humid Sunday morning, I found myself standing before this splendid church, my eyes drawn to its towering spire that seemed to touch the very heavens. I had always admired the beauty of the building from afar but had never ventured inside. Today, something compelled me to step through the towering wooden doors, beneath the stone archway, and into the sacred interior.

The moment I crossed the threshold, my breath caught in my throat. The sight that greeted me was nothing short of breathtaking. Sunlight filtered through magnificent stained glass windows, casting patterns of colored light across the polished wooden pews and mosaic-tiled floor. The air was thick with the scent of polished wood, candles, and ancient secrets.

As I walked down the central aisle, my gaze was drawn to the stained glass windows that lined both sides of the church. Each window was a work of art, depicting scenes from biblical stories and saints in vivid, intricate detail. The colors were so vibrant, the craftsmanship so exquisite, that I felt a deep sense of awe and reverence wash over me.

But then, as I reached the middle of the aisle, something unexpected caught my eye. Among the magnificent windows, there was one that stood out, not for its beauty, but for its imperfection. Right in the center of a breathtaking scene of angels and archangels, a tiny crack marred the glass. It was as if someone had taken a fine crystal vase and struck it with a single, precise blow.

I couldn't tear my eyes away from that crack. I stood there, contemplating it, wondering how something so flawless could bear such a glaring fault. The longer I stared, the more the crack seemed to grow in significance, overshadowing the surrounding beauty.

It was then that a soft voice broke my reverie. "Beautiful, isn't it?" I turned to find an elderly woman standing beside me, a warm smile on her face. She was dressed in a simple, well-worn coat, her gray hair neatly pulled back into a bun. I was also amazed that she spoke English so well in this small Spanish speaking country.

"Yes, it is," I replied, my eyes still fixed on the cracked glass.

The woman followed my gaze. "Ah, I see you've noticed the crack. It's been there for as long as I can remember."

I nodded. "It's just...strange. With all this beauty around, it's hard not to focus on that one imperfection."

The woman chuckled softly. "Isn't that how life often is? We're surrounded by beauty, by goodness, by countless blessings, and yet we fixate on our flaws and imperfections."

I turned to the woman, intrigued by her words. "What do you mean?"

The woman gestured toward the stained-glass window. "That crack represents the human condition. We all have our cracks, our imperfections, our faults. But they don't define us. They're just a part of the whole. Just like that cracked glass is still a part of this magnificent window, you are still a part of this beautiful world."

As I absorbed the woman's wisdom, I realized the truth in her words. How often had I focused on my own flaws, whether it was my crooked teeth or the scar on my eyebrow from a childhood accident? How often had I judged others for their imperfections, failing to see the beauty and goodness that lay beneath the surface?

The woman continued, "You see, my dear, it's easy to get caught up in the cracks, both in ourselves and in others. But when we do that, we miss out on the beauty that surrounds us. We miss out on the warmth of human connection, the richness of life's experiences, and the joy of embracing our uniqueness."

I nodded, my heart feeling lighter with each passing moment. I realized that I had been so focused on the cracked glass that I had almost missed the beauty of the entire church, the stories it held, and the people who gathered within its walls.

The woman smiled at my realization. "Remember, my dear, no one is perfect. We all have our cracks, but it's those very imperfections that make us unique and beautiful in our own way. Instead of dwelling on the cracks, let us focus on the light that shines through them, for that is where the true beauty lies."

I thanked the woman for her wisdom and watched as she slowly made her way down the aisle, disappearing into the warm embrace of the church. Left alone with the stained glass, I felt a newfound sense of peace and gratitude wash over me.

As I left the church that day, I carried with me not only the memory of the cracked stained glass but also a profound understanding of the beauty that exists in imperfection. I knew that, just like the church, I was a mosaic of experiences, flaws, and strengths, and that it was in embracing all of these facets that I would truly experience the richness of life and the depth of human connection. Getting to know our own faults is important and it helps us to stop focusing on others faults; instead looking at the good in each other and building on that beauty and uniqueness that makes us who we really are.

GIVING

In the annals of history, there's a story that has resonated across generations—a story of plenty and famine, wisdom and foresight. It's the tale of Joseph and the seven years of plenty and the seven years of lean in ancient Egypt. But this isn't just a tale of ancient times; it's a timeless parable that carries a profound lesson about giving and the consequences of our actions.

In this chapter, we'll delve into the wisdom of Joseph's story, explore the concept of giving, and discover why practicing generosity enriches not only our lives but also the lives of those around us.

Picture a land blessed by nature, where the fields yield bountiful harvests year after year. This was the Egypt of Joseph's time—a time of abundance, prosperity, and overflowing granaries. These years of plenty, known as the "seven fat years," were a period of unparalleled plenty.

But what's intriguing is not just the abundance itself but how it was managed. During these years, Joseph, with his foresight and wisdom, advised the Pharaoh to store up a significant portion of the harvest to prepare for the inevitable lean years that would follow. The people of Egypt diligently followed this advice, filling their storehouses with grain.

Now, let's pause for a moment and imagine an alternate scenario. What if, during these fat years, some individuals had chosen not to store anything? What if they had simply reveled in the abundance, indulging in every pleasure without a thought for the future? Indeed, it's likely that they would have felt remorse when the lean years arrived.

The seven years of lean, often referred to as the "seven lean years," came as predicted. Famine swept across Egypt and the surrounding lands. People began to suffer, and their storehouses dwindled. In this time of scarcity, the wisdom of Joseph's plan became evident.

Those who had stored diligently had a lifeline—a reserve of grain to see them through the tough times. They could feed their families, help their neighbors, and contribute to their communities. But what about those who had chosen not to store during the fat years? They found themselves in a dire situation, dependent on the generosity of others, struggling to make ends meet, and haunted by regret.

The Lessons of Joseph's Story

Joseph's story teaches us several lessons about giving, foresight, and the consequences of our actions:

Foresight and Preparedness: Just as Joseph advised Pharaoh to prepare for the lean years during the fat years, we, too, should exercise foresight in our lives. This means planning, saving, and being prepared for the uncertainties that lie ahead. It's not about being pessimistic; it's about being responsible.

The Value of Generosity: The people who stored grain during the fat years not only secured their own well-being but also had the capacity to help others. Generosity isn't just about giving when times are good; it's about being able to lend a hand when others are in need.

Regret and Remorse: Regret is a powerful emotion. Those who failed to prepare during the fat years likely felt deep remorse when the lean years arrived. It's a reminder that our actions, or inactions, have consequences, and it's far better to act with wisdom and foresight than to rue missed opportunities.

Now, let's reflect on a universal truth: abundance can be deceptive. When life is overflowing with riches, be they material or emotional, it's easy to become complacent, even greedy. We might indulge in the pleasures of the moment without considering the future. We might forget the value of preparation and giving.

Imagine those who enjoyed the fat years to the fullest, reveling in their abundance without a thought for tomorrow. They might have grown fatter, metaphorically speaking, as they accumulated pleasures and possessions. But the truth is that these pleasures, if not shared or preserved, are fleeting. They are like grains of sand slipping through our fingers, leaving only the memory of their touch.

So, what does all of this have to do with giving? Everything.

Giving isn't just about what we offer to others; it's also about what we give to ourselves—wisdom, compassion, and a sense of purpose. When we give, we become stewards of abundance. We recognize that the blessings we enjoy, whether they are material wealth or the richness of relationships, are meant to be shared and preserved.

In the lean years, we often learn more about ourselves and the world than in the fat years. Scarcity has a way of teaching us resilience, resourcefulness, and empathy. It reminds us of our interdependence and the importance of community.

Likewise, when we encounter challenges in our lives, whether they are financial setbacks, health issues, or personal crises, it's an opportunity to grow and learn. It's a reminder to reach out, not just for help, but to offer help where we can. It took me a long time to realize that it is okay to ask for help, people truly do love to help. It is our EGO's that whisper to our inner thoughts that we are weak for asking and this is the furthest thing from the truth.

Greed is a sneaky adversary. It whispers in our ear during the fat years, encouraging us to accumulate more and more, often at the expense of others. It tricks us into believing that our worth is measured by the size of our possessions or bank accounts.

But the truth is that greed is a hollow companion. It may provide temporary satisfaction, but it leaves a void in the soul. The pursuit of endless wealth or pleasure rarely leads to lasting happiness. It's like trying to fill a bucket with a hole at the bottom; no matter how much you pour in, it will never be enough.

On the flip side, giving brings a different kind of abundance—the abundance of joy, fulfillment, and connection. It's the joy of knowing that your actions have made a positive difference in someone's life. It's the fulfillment that comes from being a force for good in the world. And it's the deep sense of connection to humanity that reminds us we are all in this together.

Giving doesn't have to be grand or extravagant. It can be as simple as a smile, a kind word, or a helping hand. It can be the act of sharing your time, knowledge, or resources with someone in need. It can be the decision to forgive, to let go of resentment, and to offer understanding.

When we give, we create a ripple effect. Our acts of kindness and generosity inspire others to do the same. It's like dropping a pebble into a pond—the ripples spread far and wide, touching lives we may never even know.

Think back to Joseph's story. The act of storing grain during the fat years not only saved the lives of those who prepared but also had a cascading effect on the entire community. It created a network of support and goodwill that transcended the years of plenty and scarcity.

What kind of legacy do you want to leave behind? Do you want to be remembered for your wealth and possessions, or for the impact you had on the lives of others? The legacy of giving is enduring; it outlives us and continues to influence generations to come.

Consider the great philanthropists and humanitarians of history—individuals like Mother Teresa, Mahatma Gandhi, and Nelson Mandela. Their legacies are not defined by their personal wealth or fame but by their unwavering commitment to giving and making the world a better place.

So, how do we embrace a life of giving? It begins with a shift in perspective. It starts with recognizing that true abundance is not measured by what we accumulate for ourselves but by what we share with others.

Here are some practical steps to cultivate a spirit of giving in your life:

Practice Gratitude: Begin each day by acknowledging the blessings in your life, no matter how small they may seem. Gratitude is the gateway to generosity.

Start Small: You don't need to make grand gestures to give. Start with small acts of kindness and build from there. Hold the door for someone, offer a listening ear, or donate to a local charity.

Give Your Time: Time is one of the most precious gifts you can offer. Volunteer your time to a cause you're passionate about. Whether it's mentoring a young person, helping at a local shelter, or participating in a community cleanup, your time can make a significant difference and build memories for you and all who you encounter during volunteering.

Share Your Knowledge: If you possess expertise in a particular field, consider sharing your knowledge with others. Offer to mentor someone or volunteer to teach a workshop, your writings, or teaching a class.

Practice Forgiveness: Forgiveness is a powerful form of giving, both to others and to yourself. Holding onto grudges and resentment only weighs you down. Let go and make room for healing.

Give Without Expectation: True giving is unconditional. When you give without expecting anything in return, you experience the purest form of generosity.

Teach by Example: If you have children or influence over young minds, remember that you're teaching them about giving through your actions. Be a role model for generosity.

Seek Out Opportunities: Keep an eye out for opportunities to give, whether it's supporting a friend in need, contributing to a crowdfunding campaign, or participating in a community event.

The Gift That Keeps Giving

As you embark on your journey of giving, you'll discover that the act of giving is, in itself, a gift. It's a gift to the recipient, a gift to your own soul, and a gift to the world.

When you give, you create a positive feedback loop of kindness and connection. You become part of a larger tapestry of human compassion, where each thread, no matter how small, contributes to the beauty of the whole.

In the end, the seven fat years of indulgence and abundance may indeed be enjoyable, but they are fleeting. They are moments in time that will become memories. The seven lean years, however, are the crucible in which our character is forged. They are the times when we learn the true value of wisdom, foresight, and giving.

So, my dear reader, as you reflect on Joseph's story and the lessons it imparts, remember that your life is a tapestry of moments, and how you choose to weave them matters. Embrace the spirit of giving, and you'll find that in the lean years and the fat years alike, you are creating a legacy of abundance—one that transcends time and leaves a lasting mark on the world.

Now here is another version of the story to show a few more lessons I have learned in all my studies of learning about my true self. In a distant land, there once existed a kingdom ruled by a wicked and miserly king named Balthazar. His rule was marked by cruelty, greed, and a relentless pursuit of power. He cared not for the well-being of his subjects, but only for his own riches and comfort.

The kingdom, once known for its prosperity and unity, had fallen into a state of despair. The people were burdened with heavy taxes, while King Balthazar lived in luxury. His coffers overflowed with gold, while his subjects struggled to make ends meet. Misery hung over the land like a dark cloud.

In the early years of his reign, King Balthazar experienced what he called "the seven fat years." These were years of unparalleled abundance and prosperity for the kingdom. The coffers filled to the brim, and the king reveled in his newfound wealth.

During these years, King Balthazar had a choice. He could have used the kingdom's riches to alleviate the suffering of his people, to invest in education, infrastructure, and healthcare. He could have fostered a sense of unity and well-being among his subjects.

But, King Balthazar's heart was as cold as his gold. He squandered the kingdom's wealth on extravagant feasts, luxurious palaces, and lavish entertainments. His subjects, though they toiled tirelessly, saw little benefit from the riches of their land.

As King Balthazar reveled in his wealth during the fat years, a wise sage named Seraphina arrived at the outskirts of the kingdom. Seraphina was known far and wide for her wisdom and her ability to see beyond the material world. She sensed the imbalance in the kingdom and knew that the lean years were approaching.

She decided to speak to the people, to offer them guidance and hope. Seraphina gathered the villagers in the town square and began to share her wisdom.

"Dear people," she said, her voice filled with compassion, "I see lean years on the horizon. The abundance you've enjoyed may soon give way to scarcity. But fear not, for there is a path to prosperity even in the leanest of times."

The villagers listened intently as Seraphina spoke of the importance of giving, of sharing their resources, and of caring for one another. She spoke of the ripple effect of kindness and generosity and how it had the power to transform not only individual lives but entire communities.

King Balthazar, ever watchful of his wealth, overheard Seraphina's words. He dismissed her as a mere beggar and ordered her banished from the kingdom. But Seraphina's words had already taken root in the hearts of the people, and her message of giving and kindness began to spread.

As the lean years descended upon the kingdom, King Balthazar's wealth began to dwindle. His palaces lost their luster, and his feasts grew meager. The people, once resigned to their fate, began to look out for one another. They shared what little they had and helped those in need.

Meanwhile, King Balthazar's misery grew like a cancer in his heart. He hoarded his remaining wealth, convinced that he could hold onto it until the lean years passed. But the more he clung to his riches, the more they slipped through his fingers.

In the midst of the lean years, a remarkable transformation took place in the kingdom. The people, bound by a sense of community and compassion, found strength in their unity. They discovered that their capacity for love and generosity was boundless.

Parents shared their meager meals with their children. Neighbors helped one another repair their homes. The sick were cared for, and the elderly were comforted. The kingdom, once marked by misery, was now illuminated by the unconditional love of its people.

Seraphina, though banished, continued to watch over the kingdom from afar. She saw the people's acts of kindness and marveled at their resilience. She knew that their love for one another was a powerful force, capable of transforming even the darkest of times.

As the lean years stretched on, King Balthazar's despair deepened. He watched with envy as the people of his kingdom found solace in their acts of giving and love. His heart, long hardened by greed, began to crack.

One day, as he walked through the now-humble streets of his kingdom, King Balthazar witnessed a child sharing his last piece of bread with a hungry stranger. He saw the tears of gratitude in the stranger's eyes and heard the laughter of the child. Something stirred within him.

King Balthazar, burdened by the weight of his own misery, approached Seraphina, who had returned to the kingdom's outskirts. With tears in his eyes, he spoke, "I have lived my life in pursuit of wealth and power, and it has brought me nothing but misery. I see now that true richness lies in the love and kindness we share with one another."

With Seraphina's guidance, King Balthazar began to make amends. He donated his remaining wealth to the people, investing in the well-being of the kingdom. He worked side by side with his subjects, helping to rebuild the community and strengthen the bonds of unity.

As the lean years gradually gave way to a new era, the kingdom underwent a remarkable transformation. It became known not for the wealth of its ruler but for the generosity and love of its people. The legacy of the lean years endured, serving as a reminder that true prosperity lay in giving, not in hoarding.

The once-miserable kingdom had become a place of happiness and harmony. Its people had learned the value of unconditional love—the love that knows no boundaries, no conditions, and no limits. It was a love that had the power to heal wounds, bridge divides, and transform a kingdom of misery into a kingdom of joy.

In the end, the tale of King Balthazar's kingdom serves as a powerful reminder of the consequences of greed and the transformative power of giving and love. It illustrates that evil, characterized by cruelty, can only lead to misery—both for the one who harbors it and for those affected by it.

But it also underscores the resilience of the human spirit and the capacity for change and redemption. King Balthazar's transformation, driven by a newfound understanding of the importance of love and giving, shows that even the darkest hearts can find their way back to the light.

The story also echoes the timeless truth that unconditional love, like the love of our children, our brothers and sisters, and our parents, is the purest form of love. It's a love that can be tested by the trials of life but can never be broken. It's a love that binds us together, transcending differences and hardships. Love always wins, love is a light that will dim any darkness. Change is brought to all of us by example, not just words. The king needed to see the changes around him in order to break his evil ways, this is so true for all of us.

So, let us take this tale to heart and remember that our actions have the power to shape our lives and the lives of those around us. Let us learn from the mistakes of King Balthazar and the wisdom of Seraphina, embracing a life of giving and unconditional love. For in doing so, we can transform our own kingdoms, no matter how small or large, into places of abundance, joy, and real enduring love.

ALL HUMANS ARE WEAK

Human beings, with all their achievements and aspirations, are not immune to weakness - an inclination towards anger and pettiness over seemingly insignificant matters. This frailty of our inner selves often remains hidden beneath the veneer of our public personas, but it's a part of the human experience that deserves careful examination.

The essence of our daily battles often lies in the clash between our desires and our ability to control them. It's a struggle that we, as individuals and as a society, need to confront honestly. We often refuse to acknowledge our weaknesses, blaming external circumstances or other people for our discontent. It's easier to point fingers than to turn inward and confront the demons within us.

Think about the last time you got irritated over something trivial - perhaps a slow-moving line at the coffee shop or a coworker's minor mistake. These moments of frustration are, in essence, a manifestation of our inner frailties. We give in to these base emotions more often than we'd like to admit, and it leaves us feeling drained, even though the issues at hand are often insignificant in the grand scheme of life.

The question then becomes, how do we overcome these weaknesses? How do we learn to control our desires, temper our anger, and rise above pettiness? The answer, it seems, lies in the power of pure intentions - in choosing the path of always helping others and doing the right thing.

Consider this: when we act with pure intentions, our focus shifts away from our own desires and towards the betterment of others. We begin to empathize, to understand the struggles and challenges faced by those around us. In this shift, we find a greater purpose beyond the pursuit of personal gratification. We recognize that the fleeting satisfaction of getting our way in a minor dispute pales in comparison to the fulfillment derived from helping others and doing what is right.

The key is to cultivate mindfulness - to pause and reflect before we react. This pause allows us to distance ourselves from the immediate emotional response and evaluate the situation rationally. It's a practice that requires patience and self-awareness but can yield profound results. By recognizing that our desires are often transient and that anger over petty matters is counterproductive, we can start to let go of these negative emotions.

Moreover, when we choose the path of helping others and doing the correct thing, we set an example for those around us. Our actions have a ripple effect, inspiring positive change in our communities and, ultimately, in society as a whole. The more we practice this, the more we create an environment where kindness and empathy become the norm rather than the exception.

In acknowledging our weaknesses and striving to overcome them, start on a journey of self-discovery and personal growth. By focusing on pure intentions, we shift our perspective from the mundane to the meaningful. We find strength in vulnerability, resilience in compassion, and true contentment in helping others and doing what is right.

The path to conquering our inner frailties may not be easy, but it is a journey well worth taking. It's a journey that has the power to transform not only ourselves but also the world around us, creating a more harmonious and empathetic society where petty matters hold no sway over our collective spirit.

In our fast-paced world, it's all too common to find ourselves seeking solace in our desires and weaknesses. Stress, frustration, and the chaos of daily life can lead us down the path of over-indulgence—whether it's reaching for that extra drink, lighting up a cigarette, or diving headfirst into a bag of chips. But what if I told you there's a way to naturally shed these habits and find balance by focusing on the positives in life?

Our desires and weaknesses often emerge as coping mechanisms when we feel overwhelmed. They provide a sense of comfort, a momentary distraction from life's challenges. However, this comfort is temporary, leaving us feeling worse than before, trapped in a cycle of unhealthy habits.

The key to breaking free from this cycle lies in redirecting our focus towards the positives. Instead of seeking refuge in self-destructive behaviors, we can learn to find solace and strength in our thoughts, goals, and the abundance of positive aspects in our lives.

1. **Identify Your Triggers**: Start by identifying the triggers that lead you towards those negative habits. Is it stress at work? Relationship problems? Boredom? Understanding the root causes of your desires and weaknesses is the first step towards addressing them.

2. **Set Clear Goals**: Establishing clear, achievable goals in various aspects of your life can help you regain control. These goals give you something positive to focus on, redirecting your energy away from destructive habits. Whether it's a fitness goal, a career aspiration, or a personal development target, having something to work toward can be highly motivating.

3. **Embrace Mindfulness**: Mindfulness, the practice of being present in the moment without judgment, can be a powerful tool for overcoming desires and weaknesses. When you become aware of your impulses and feelings, you can pause and choose a healthier response. Instead of reaching for a cigarette, you might opt for a few deep breaths or a brisk walk.

4. **Cultivate Gratitude**: Gratitude is a transformative force. Each day, take a moment to reflect on the positive aspects of your life. It could be as simple as appreciating a beautiful sunrise, a supportive friend, or your own accomplishments. Gratitude shifts your focus away from what you lack and towards what you have.

5. **Seek Support**: You don't have to navigate this journey alone. Reach out to friends, family, or even a therapist who can offer guidance and support. Sharing your goals and progress with others not only holds you accountable but also reinforces your commitment to change.

6. **Replace Bad Habits with Healthy Ones**: As you build a positive, goal-oriented mindset, you'll naturally find that your bad habits begin to lose their grip on you. Consider replacing them with healthier alternatives, like exercise, meditation, or pursuing a new hobby.

7. **Celebrate Small Wins**: Recognize and celebrate every small victory along the way. Every time you make a choice that aligns with your positive goals, it's a step towards a balanced, healthier life.

Balancing our lives by focusing on the positives isn't about deprivation or forcing change; it's about nurturing your inner strength and resilience. Over time, as you align your thoughts and actions with your goals, you'll discover that the desires and weaknesses that once held you captive naturally fade away. It's a journey that brings not only personal growth but also a deeper appreciation for the beauty and positivity that life has to offer.

TALK IS CHEAP

In the grand theater of life, where every individual plays a leading role, talk is the understudy that's always waiting in the wings. We are, by nature, a species that revels in words, a relentless stream of chatter that flows ceaselessly from our lips. Yet, despite the overuse of words that defines our existence, it's no secret that talk is, indeed, cheap.

Our daily existence is punctuated by countless interactions with others, brief encounters that flicker like snapshots in the film reel of our lives. In these fleeting moments, we are quick to judge, to form snap impressions based on appearances, tones, and choice phrases. Why do we do this? Why do we feel compelled to make judgments, to size up others with such haste?

This instinctual reaction is, in part, a coping mechanism. We are constantly bombarded with stimuli from our environment, and making quick judgments is a way to filter and process this overwhelming amount of information. In the blink of an eye, we assess whether someone is a potential friend or foe, trustworthy or untrustworthy. It's a survival tactic etched deep into our evolutionary history, designed to help us navigate a world filled with uncertainties.

Yet, beneath this veneer of quick judgments lies a complexity of emotions. While we may be adept at sizing up others, we often struggle when it comes to understanding ourselves. Our innate fears and insecurities can lead us to make choices that seem paradoxical.

One such paradox is our fear of success. It may sound odd, even counterintuitive, but it's a very real and potent force in our lives. We fear success because it carries with it the weight of expectations and responsibilities. Achieving success means stepping into a new spotlight, and with it comes the glaring fear of failure under that intense scrutiny.

In a world where talk is indeed cheap, our actions speak volumes. We may harbor dreams and ambitions, but we often self-sabotage out of the fear that success will expose our vulnerabilities. We fear that others will see through our façade, that we'll be unable to meet the high standards we've set for ourselves.

To compensate for our fears and insecurities, we adopt a facade of strength. We pretend to be tougher than we are, projecting an image of confidence even when we feel anything but. This facade can serve as armor, protecting us from the judgments of others and bolstering our own sense of self-worth.

We've all heard the phrase, "fake it till you make it," and in many ways, it encapsulates this human tendency. We act as if we have all the answers, as if we are impervious to doubt and fear. We believe that if we can just convince others—and perhaps ourselves—that we are strong and capable, we can overcome any obstacle.

Yet, there is a price to pay for this pretense. As we build walls of strength around ourselves, we distance ourselves from our true selves. We become prisoners of the image we've crafted, trapped in a performance that never ends. The more we pretend, the further we drift from authenticity, and the more we lose touch with our own vulnerabilities and humanity.

In the end, we must remember that talk is indeed cheap. Words can be a powerful tool, but they are but the surface ripples of a vast sea of thoughts, fears, and desires. To understand ourselves and others, we must be willing to dive deeper, to look beyond the facade, and to embrace the complexities that make us human. Only then can we begin to unravel the paradoxes of judgment, fear, and success that shape our lives.

Here is a short story about how I taught a young manager to be more authentic and helped him to build a better company (to ensure the privacy and protect the individual involved, names in the story have been changed):

In the bustling heart of the city, there was a young man named Alex. Fresh out of college and never had a professional job, he had recently landed a job as a salesman and manager at a successful firm. Bright, ambitious, and eager to make his mark, Alex was a quick learner, but he had a peculiar habit that soon caught the attention of his seasoned colleague, David.

David was a man of experience, a veteran of the business world who had seen trends come and go, and had witnessed the rise and fall of countless companies. He had a keen eye for authenticity, a trait that had served him well over the years. It wasn't long before he noticed something about Alex that intrigued him.

Alex, it seemed, had an insatiable appetite for complex, professional-sounding words. He constantly memorized jargon and industry buzzwords, deploying them with flourish in his interactions with clients. In meetings and presentations, he would pepper his speech with phrases like "synergy," "paradigm shift," and "value-added proposition." He believed that using such words would make him sound smarter and more like an expert, earning him the respect of clients and colleagues alike.

One day, after a particularly verbose client presentation, David invited Alex for a coffee break. They found themselves sitting in a cozy corner of a nearby café, sipping on steaming cups of coffee as the city buzzed around them.

"Alex," David began, his voice measured and calm, "I've been observing your presentations, and I couldn't help but notice your fondness for those big words."

Alex, his expression a mix of surprise and curiosity, nodded. "Yes, David, I believe it makes me sound more professional, more like an expert."

David leaned in, his eyes locking onto Alex's. "Let me share a secret with you, my friend. In my years of business, I've learned that clients don't always want to hear those big words. What they truly want is authenticity."

Alex frowned, puzzled. "Authenticity? What do you mean?"

David smiled, his eyes crinkling at the corners with the wisdom of age. "Clients want to connect with someone who believes in their service, someone who speaks from the heart. When you use those words, it can come across as a smokescreen, as if you're trying to hide something. Clients can see through that."

Alex pondered this for a moment. "But I thought using those words would make me sound more knowledgeable."

"Knowledge is essential," David agreed, "but it should be conveyed sincerely. You see, people do business with people they trust. And trust is built on authenticity. If you believe in your service and can communicate that belief honestly, clients will trust you."

As the weeks passed, Alex took David's words to heart. He began to strip away the layers of jargon, replacing them with genuine passion and confidence in the services he offered. It wasn't long before clients started responding differently. They could sense the sincerity in Alex's voice, the authenticity in his words.

With time, Alex realized that talk was indeed cheap when it lacked authenticity. He had been so focused on appearing knowledgeable that he had forgotten the most crucial element in business —building trust. Through his newfound authenticity, he not only gained the trust of clients but also deepened his own understanding of the industry. His confidence grew, and his success followed suit.

In the end, David's wisdom had shown Alex that it wasn't the words that mattered most in business; it was the genuine belief in the value of the service and the authenticity in how it was presented. And as Alex continued to grow in his career, he knew that this lesson would remain with him, a testament to the power of authenticity in a world where talk was indeed cheap.

KEEP DISCOURAGEMENT OUT OF
YOUR LIFE

Have you ever paused to contemplate your existence in the grand scheme of the universe? Why are you here, on this planet, at this precise moment in time? These existential questions can be both profound and perplexing, often leading us to explore the depths of our purpose and significance. However, in our journey through life, we are bound to encounter moments of discouragement and self-doubt.

Life is a rollercoaster of highs and lows, a turbulent journey that we all must navigate. At times, it may seem that discouragement is an unwelcome companion, always lurking around the corner. It's during these moments of self-reflection and vulnerability that the seeds of doubt can take root in our minds.

The battle against discouragement is a fierce one. It's a battle against our own inner demons, against the negative thoughts that can erode our self-worth and confidence. It's a battle against the creeping darkness that seeks to envelop our hearts.

The devil, in many belief systems, is often described as a malevolent force that seeks to sow discord and discontent. In our daily lives, this malevolence manifests as doubt, fear, and self-criticism. It's the voice that whispers in our ears, telling us that we're not good enough, that we're unworthy of happiness and success.

This insidious influence can lead us down a path of self-destruction if we allow it. It's essential to recognize when these negative thoughts creep in and to actively combat them. Remember, you are not alone in this struggle. We all grapple with these inner demons from time to time.

In the face of discouragement, it's tempting to harbor feelings of resentment and seek revenge against those we perceive as responsible for our distress. Yet, revenge is a double-edged sword. It may offer a fleeting sense of satisfaction, but it ultimately poisons our own hearts.

Revenge is the embodiment of hatred, a venom that consumes us from within. It drags us down to the same level as those we wish to harm. It shackles us to the past, preventing us from moving forward and finding true happiness. In the end, revenge is a futile endeavor that brings more harm than healing.

The joys and triumphs of yesterday are etched in our memories, but they are but a chapter in the book of our lives. What truly matters is the choices we make today and the direction in which we decide to steer our future.

Our thoughts are the compass that guides us forward. When discouragement knocks on our door, we have the power to choose how we respond. We can embrace resilience and optimism, seeking solutions to our challenges, or we can succumb to despair.

In our darkest moments, it's crucial to remind ourselves of our inherent worth and the potential that resides within us. We are here on this planet at this time for a reason, and that reason is rooted in our capacity to learn, grow, and make a positive impact.

Discouragement is a formidable adversary, but it is not invincible. By recognizing the negative influences in our thoughts, by letting go of the toxic allure of revenge, and by embracing the power of choice, we can keep discouragement at bay.

Remember, life is a journey of self-discovery and growth. The joys of yesterday are but stepping stones on this path. It's the choices we make today that will shape our tomorrows. So, choose resilience, choose optimism, and choose to nurture the light within you, for it is in these choices that we find the strength to overcome life's trials and tribulations.

In revisiting my own experience of being fired because it was such a traumatic time for me, I hope to emphasize the importance of keeping discouragement at bay in our lives:

My life had been a tale of dedication and hard work. For years, I had poured my heart and soul into a job that I believed was my calling. The company had been my second home, the colleagues my extended family and actual family. But despite my years of unwavering dedication, the day came when I received the unexpected news – I was being let go from my job that I had worked most of my adult life.

The shock and dismay that accompanied the termination were palpable. I had given my all to this company, and I had believed that my loyalty would be rewarded. Instead, I found myself facing an uncertain future, burdened by discouragement and resentment.

In the days that followed, as I packed up my belongings, I couldn't help but feel a sense of betrayal. I questioned my worth and the value of my years of dedication. It was a dark period, a time when discouragement threatened to cast a long shadow over my life.

But I was not one to be defeated easily. I had spent years reading thousands of historical and spiritual books, attending classes, and seeking wisdom from gurus. It was during this difficult period that I realized the true power of forgiveness.

Forgiveness, I understood, was not just about letting go of the anger and resentment towards my former employer and father figure; it was about freeing myself from the chains of bitterness. I chose to forgive, not because it condoned the actions of my employer, but because it liberated me from the burden of carrying that anger in my heart.

With forgiveness came a sense of hope. I realized that by forgiving others and praying for their improvement, I could transform my own journey. I understood that we are all on unique paths, and sometimes, the actions of others are a reflection of their own struggles and limitations.

My prayers shifted from bitterness to hope. I prayed not for revenge but for enlightenment, not for retribution but for growth. I hoped that my former employer and colleagues would find the clarity and wisdom to create a better workplace for those who remained.

As the weeks turned into months, my life began to change in ways I could never have imagined. The time I was given by leaving a place where I was not meant to be allowed me to explore new horizons. I rekindled old passions, discovered new interests, and spent more quality time with my family.

The discouragement that once clouded my days had been replaced by a sense of joy and purpose. I understood that I had been released from a job that was not aligned with my true path, and this liberation had set me on a journey of self-discovery and fulfillment.

My story serves as a testament to the transformative power of forgiveness and hope. By choosing to forgive and pray for others, I not only freed myself from the shackles of discouragement but also embarked on a new path filled with joy and fulfillment.

In the end, I realized that life's twists and turns often lead us to where we are destined to be. It's in the moments of darkness and uncertainty that we have the opportunity to rediscover our true selves and embrace the beauty of the journey. My journey is a reminder that even in the face of discouragement, there is always a path to redemption, joy, and a brighter future. Just be open to learning and keep discouragement out of your life.

LOVE YOUR NEIGHBORS

How many times have we walked into a room of strangers and felt the mood of the room to be ice cold? It's a scenario we've all experienced at some point in our lives. You enter a room filled with people you've never met before, and the atmosphere is as chilly as an arctic breeze. You can sense the tension in the air, the discomfort in people's body language, and the guarded expressions on their faces. It's a situation that can make even the most confident among us feel a little anxiety.

The aura given off by the people in the room may seem unbearable. As you navigate this room full of strangers, you might be tempted to write off these people as unfriendly or unapproachable. It's easy to make snap judgments about their character based on their initial demeanor. After all, humans are wired to quickly assess threats and protect themselves. But what if, instead of reacting defensively, we took a moment to consider what might be causing this icy aura.

It's essential to recognize that every person in that room, just like you, desires respect, acceptance, and understanding. It's a fundamental human need to be acknowledged and valued by our peers. The icy exterior you perceive may be a defense mechanism, a shield they've put up to protect themselves from rejection or judgment. In their hearts, they yearn for the same warmth and connection that you do.

Now, this is where empathy comes into play. Understanding that people have different ways of seeking respect and acceptance can transform how we perceive those around us. Some might be extroverted and outgoing, trying to win admiration through humor and charm. Others might be introverted and reserved, preferring to earn respect through competence and dedication. And then there are those who may seem aloof or defensive, but deep down, they are just as vulnerable as anyone else.

The age-old wisdom of "Love your neighbor as yourself" takes on a profound meaning in situations like these. It doesn't just mean being polite or civil; it means extending empathy and kindness even when faced with apparent hostility. It means recognizing the humanity in every person you meet, regardless of their initial demeanor. It means understanding that beneath the surface, we are all striving for the same basic human needs: love, belonging, and respect.

Perhaps one of the most significant barriers to building connections with others is the desire to prove ourselves superior. We live in a competitive world, where the pursuit of success often overshadows the value of human connection. When we constantly compare ourselves to others, striving to be "better," we inadvertently promote self-centeredness. We lose sight of the fact that life is not a zero-sum game, and we can all thrive together.

So, the next time you find yourself in a room filled with strangers exuding an icy aura, remember this: behind those facades are individuals with their own insecurities, fears, and desires. Instead of allowing their demeanor to deter you, be the one who breaks the ice. Extend a hand in friendship, offer a smile, or simply take a moment to listen. You might be surprised by the warmth that can emerge when you approach others with empathy and a genuine desire to connect. In doing so, you not only thaw the icy mood of the room but also contribute to the creation of a more compassionate and understanding world.

Judging others is a natural human inclination. It's a mechanism we've developed over time as a way to quickly assess situations and protect ourselves from potential threats. However, while judgment can sometimes be a useful tool for survival, it can also be a significant barrier to understanding and empathy when misused or overemphasized. The key here is to recognize that we are all guilty of passing judgments on others, but we should strive to look deeper, beyond the surface, into their intentions and individuality. We should avoid judging others based on attributes such as nationality, sexuality, or any other superficial characteristic.

Every day, we encounter many people from diverse backgrounds, each with their own unique stories and experiences. It's all too easy to glance at someone and immediately categorize them based on their appearance, their accent, or their lifestyle. We make snap judgments about their character, their values, and their intentions. These judgments can be influenced by stereotypes, biases, and preconceived notions, often perpetuated by the media or societal norms, or even past experiences with other people.

Passing judgments based on nationality, sexuality, or other superficial attributes can have bad consequences. It can lead to discrimination, prejudice, and harmful stereotypes. When we judge others solely by their external characteristics, we deny them the opportunity to be seen as individuals with unique experiences, dreams, and intentions. We rob ourselves of the chance to learn from their perspectives and enrich our own lives through diverse interactions.

The path to greater understanding and empathy begins with a simple shift in mindset: looking beyond the surface. Instead of assuming we know someone based on their nationality, sexuality, or any other characteristic, let's take a step back and ask questions. Let's engage in open conversations and actively listen to their stories. Let's seek to understand their intentions, values, and dreams, recognizing that these attributes are far more complex and varied than we might initially perceive.

Empathy is a powerful force that can help us break free from the confines of judgment. It involves putting ourselves in someone else's shoes and striving to understand their experiences and emotions. When we practice empathy, we begin to see the world from multiple perspectives, fostering a sense of connection and unity rather than division. Empathy helps us realize that people of all nationalities, sexualities, and backgrounds share similar hopes, fears, and desires for a better life.

By reframing our approach to others and avoiding judgments based on superficial characteristics, we contribute to a more inclusive and equal society. We create spaces where people feel valued for who they are as individuals, not reduced to stereotypes. In doing so, we challenge discriminatory attitudes and work towards dismantling the barriers that divide us.

In conclusion, we must acknowledge that passing judgments on others is a universal human tendency. However, we have the power to transcend these judgments by focusing on understanding people's intentions, values, and individuality. Let us commit to looking beyond the surface, embracing diversity, and cultivating empathy. By doing so, we can move toward a world where people are seen and valued for their unique qualities, free from the constraints of prejudice and bias.

MIND YOUR BUSINESS

We've all been there—sitting across from a friend or family member, eager to offer our unsolicited advice. It's a common impulse, one rooted in our desire to help and support those we care about. But sometimes, the most valuable assistance we can provide is the gift of our presence, a listening ear, and the wisdom to know when to keep our opinions to ourselves.

Nothing is much more than something, especially when it comes to giving advice to our loved ones. While our intentions may be noble, our words can often do more harm than good. What we perceive as a solution may not align with their needs or desires. What we think is best may not be what they truly want.

When someone we love comes to us with a problem, it's essential to recognize their underlying intention. In many cases, they aren't seeking immediate solutions or a list of dos and don'ts. Instead, they're looking for a safe space to express their feelings, frustrations, and fears. They want to vent, to release the pent-up emotions that have been weighing them down.

Being a good listener is an art. It requires patience, empathy, and the ability to withhold judgment. It means giving your undivided attention, without interrupting or interjecting your own experiences and opinions. It's about creating a space where the person can feel heard and understood.

"The wise man keeps his mouth shut." These ancient words carry profound meaning in the context of offering advice. Often, silence is the most powerful response we can offer. It allows the other person to process their thoughts and feelings without feeling pressured or judged. It gives them the room to arrive at their own insights and solutions.

We must remember that we do not possess all the answers. Each individual's life journey is unique, shaped by their experiences, values, and aspirations. What worked for us may not work for them. What seems obvious to us might not be so clear-cut in their situation.

Empathy is the ability to understand and share in the feelings of another. It goes beyond offering solutions; it's about connecting on an emotional level. When we practice empathy, we acknowledge the other person's pain, joy, or confusion. We validate their emotions, letting them know that what they feel matters.

Empathy bridges gaps and strengthens bonds. It fosters trust and opens the door to honest, heartfelt conversations. It allows us to support our loved ones in a way that resonates with their needs and desires, rather than imposing our own agenda.

In our eagerness to help, let's not forget the profound value of simply being there for our loved ones. Listening, withholding judgment, and offering empathy are often more powerful than providing solutions or advice. By doing so, we show that we respect their autonomy and trust their judgment.

So, the next time someone you care about comes to you with a problem, remember: they might not need you to fix it. They might only need your presence, your listening ear, and your empathy. In those moments, silence can be a great virtue, and the act of truly minding your business becomes an act of love and support.

Life has an uncanny way of teaching us the most profound lessons when we least expect it. My journey of self-discovery took an unexpected turn when I made a conscious decision to mind my own business, to respect people's privacy, and to be a source of support rather than a participant in gossip.

Growing up, I was always the curious one. I had a penchant for knowing everyone's business, a knack for picking up on the latest rumors and juicy tidbits. Gossip seemed harmless, even fun, back then. But as I got older, I began to realize the corrosive effects it could have on relationships, trust, and my own sense of self.

It was during a transformative phase of my life when I decided to make a change. I had been grappling with my own personal challenges, trying to navigate adulthood, and facing moments of self-doubt and confusion. It was precisely during this time that I learned some invaluable lessons about myself and about the power of minding my own business.

One of the first lessons I embraced was the importance of respecting people's privacy. We all have our battles, our inner demons, and our private lives. By prying into others' affairs, we not only invade their personal space but also betray their trust. When we respect their boundaries, we send a powerful message that we value and honor their individuality.

As I began to practice this newfound respect for privacy, I found that my relationships deepened. People around me began to feel more comfortable confiding in me, knowing that I would safeguard their secrets and honor their need for confidentiality. In doing so, I discovered the transformative power of trust in forging meaningful connections.

One of the most significant shifts in my life occurred when I realized that I could be a source of support for others without being a gossip. Instead of engaging in conversations that tore people down, I became a compassionate listener, a shoulder to lean on during times of distress. I discovered that being there for someone in their moments of vulnerability was not only a way to help them but also a source of personal fulfillment.

In offering genuine empathy and support, I learned to understand the intricacies of human emotions, the depth of pain and joy that we all experience. I realized that by being present for others, I could tap into my own well of empathy and compassion, making me a better, more empathetic person.

Minding my own business also taught me a great deal about integrity. I came to understand that true integrity is not just about being honest in our actions but also in our words and thoughts. It's about living in alignment with our values and principles, even when no one is watching.

By choosing to abstain from gossip and respecting the privacy of others, I strengthened my own integrity. I learned that integrity is not only about external actions but also about the choices we make in our hearts and minds. It's about being true to ourselves and upholding our values even in the face of societal pressures.

In the end, minding my own business became a journey of profound self-discovery. It taught me that by letting go of the need to know everyone's business, I could focus on understanding myself better. It allowed me to cultivate qualities like empathy, respect, and integrity that ultimately enriched my life and my relationships.

So, as I continue on this journey of self-discovery, I carry with me the lessons learned from minding my own business. I strive to be a source of support, a compassionate listener, and a guardian of trust. And in doing so, I've found that the path to self-discovery is not always about looking inward; sometimes, it's about looking outward with empathy, understanding, and a heart full of kindness.

CHAPTER SIX: SICKNESS AND DEATH

DISEASE

Disease is a multifaceted phenomenon, one that extends beyond the physical realm. It's a complex interplay of biology, environment, and emotions. In this chapter, we delve into the intriguing connection between disease, negative emotions, and the power of healing. We'll explore how emotions like anger, hate, and sadness can be contagious and detrimental to our well-being, but also how they can be transformed into sources of healing and resilience.

Negative emotions, much like infectious diseases, have the power to spread from one individual to another. It's a phenomenon that psychologists and sociologists have long studied. When we encounter someone who is angry or anxious, it often triggers a similar emotional response within us. The negativity ripples outward, affecting not only our mental state but also our physical health.

Consider a room filled with tension and anger. You can almost feel the emotional weight pressing down on you. The negative energy is heavy, and it affects everyone in the room. This emotional contagion can be insidious, leading to a cycle of escalating negativity if left unchecked.

The contagion of negative emotions will persist for eternity if we allow it to. But herein lies a crucial truth: we have the power to break this cycle. It's a choice we make every day, consciously or unconsciously. When we recognize the harmful impact of negative emotions on our well-being, we gain the motivation to put out the flames of anger and negativity.

Negative emotions, when left unchecked, can become toxic. They manifest as stress, resentment, and even physical health issues. Clinicians have indeed proven that stress is the number one killer in America. The constant barrage of stressful thoughts and emotions takes a toll on our bodies, leading to diseases like heart disease, diabetes, and more.

The Law of Attraction believes that our thoughts and emotions have a direct influence on our reality. What we focus on, consciously or unconsciously, tends to manifest in our lives. This principle underscores the importance of paying attention to our thoughts and words. When we dwell on negativity, we inadvertently attract more of the same into our lives.

It's essential, therefore, to shift our focus away from the small matters that often consume our thoughts. By practicing mindfulness and maintaining a positive outlook, we can influence our reality in a more constructive and healing way.

Elisabeth Kübler-Ross, a pioneer in the field of death and dying, described the emotional stages that both the dying and their loved ones go through: denial, anger, bargaining, depression, and acceptance. These stages illustrate the emotional rollercoaster that accompanies the experience of death and profound loss. They also underscore the notion that emotions are not just mental constructs —they have tangible effects on our physical health.

Disease is not solely about suffering; it can also serve as a catalyst for healing. When we face adversity, it forces us to confront our deepest emotions and traumas. It prompts us to seek ways to cope, adapt, and ultimately find resilience.

Embracing the power of healing involves acknowledging our emotions, both positive and negative, and channeling them in constructive ways. It means finding acceptance and meaning in our experiences, even when faced with the most challenging circumstances.

Disease is not just a physical ailment—it's an intricate interplay of body, mind, and spirit. The contagion of negative emotions reminds us of the importance of emotional hygiene and mental well-being. It calls us to break the cycle of negativity and choose healing, not only for ourselves but for the collective.

In our journey through life, we must remember the profound connection between emotions, thoughts, and our physical health. We can use this awareness to transform disease from a killer into a source of healing. By embracing acceptance, resilience, and positivity, we can chart a path toward a healthier, more fulfilling existence.

So, let us not underestimate the power of our emotions in shaping our lives. Let us mindfully choose to be sources of healing, love, and compassion, recognizing that the contagion of these positive emotions has the potential to transform our world for the better. And, in doing so, let us heed the timeless wisdom: "Never go to bed angry, for we do not know when our last day will be."

As a hospice volunteer, I have had the privilege of being with hundreds of people in their final hours, witnessing their remarkable transformations and the extraordinary strength and love they displayed as they embarked on the profound journey of transitioning from life to death.

Each of these experiences has left an indelible mark on my heart, but it was the lessons I learned from my own family that truly illuminated the path towards embracing the inevitable with grace and courage.

Hospice care, often associated with the end of life, provides a unique space where people can find comfort and support during their final days. It's a place where the focus shifts from curing illness to ensuring the highest possible quality of life in the time that remains.

In my years as a hospice volunteer, I've seen individuals at their most vulnerable and raw moments. I've observed the power of compassion, the solace of a comforting presence, and the peace that comes with letting go of fear and embracing acceptance.

One of the most remarkable aspects of my journey as a hospice volunteer has been witnessing the transformations that occur in the last hours of a person's life. There's a shift, almost palpable, as if they are shedding the burdens of this world and preparing for the next. It's a transition that can be filled with moments of both anguish and serenity.

Some patients experience profound moments of clarity and connection with loved ones, sharing stories and laughter as if time had reversed. Others find solace in solitude, quietly reflecting on their life's journey. And some, in their final moments, seem to transcend the physical realm, radiating a sense of peace that touches everyone in the room.

While I had the privilege of witnessing these incredible transformations in strangers, it was the experiences with my own family that taught me some of the most valuable lessons about life and death.

When my mother faced her final days, she did so with a grace and strength that left us all in awe. Her smile never wavered, and her love shone brightly through the pain. She reassured us that she was ready for the next stage of her journey, that she had no fear, only a sense of peaceful anticipation.

Similarly, my brother, in his last days, displayed a remarkable resilience. His humor and love remained undiminished, even as his body weakened. He brought us together, reminding us of the importance of cherishing the moments we have and letting go of the trivialities that often consume our lives.

These experiences with my mother and brother have left an enduring impression on my soul. They taught me that death is not something to be feared but rather an inevitable part of the human experience. It's a transition, a passage from one state of being to another, and it can be approached with grace, love, and acceptance.

As I reflect on the countless individuals I've been privileged to accompany on their final journey, I am filled with hope and gratitude. I hope that when my time comes, I can be as brave as they were, passing on strength, love, and reassurance to my loved ones. I hope to let them know that I am okay with the process of my body dying, for I believe that our spirits go on to the next level, whatever that may be.

In the end, my journey as a hospice volunteer has been a profound testament to the resilience of the human spirit, the power of love, and the beauty of embracing the inevitable with open hearts and open minds.

PRAY FOR THE DEAD

The loss of a loved one has a way of ushering us into a realm where the boundary between the physical and the spiritual blurs. It's a place where the whispers of departed souls linger, and where the power of prayer takes on a profound significance. For me, this journey into the world beyond began with the wisdom my father imparted - "Pray for the dead; it helps them find their way to heaven."

After my mother's passing, I often found solace in my dreams. There, in the quiet hours of the night, she would appear, dancing in our old kitchen or twirling with me by the Christmas tree. These dreams brought me comfort, an unspoken assurance that she was at peace. I would awake with a heart full of love and gratitude, convinced that she was still watching over me.

My father's passing, when I was just thirteen, left a mark on my young heart. He had always been my source of guidance and strength, and the void his absence left was immense. But one day, when I was driving home from school, in the depths of teenage melancholy, something extraordinary happened. I felt a gentle slap on my head, and I heard his voice saying, "Be happy." In that moment, I knew he had come to me in spirit, offering fatherly advice that would guide me through life's trials and tribulations.

Prayer, for me, transcends the confines of a specific house of worship or religious doctrine. Raised Roman Catholic, I have always cherished the sacred spaces of churches, where the scent of incense and the warmth of candlelight create an atmosphere of deep reverence. But I've also found profound spirituality in the quiet contemplation of nature or the stillness of my own heart.

It is said in the Bible, in John 14:20, "On that day you will realize that I am in my Father, and you are in me, and I am in you." These words, and many others, suggest a connection between the Divine and the human spirit, a union that transcends religious boundaries. In my belief, we are all one, connected by a universal thread of love and divinity. "I AM" is not just a phrase; it's a recognition that the essence of God resides within each of us.

Religions, each with their unique traditions and interpretations, offer us a diverse tapestry of spiritual wisdom. In this rich mosaic, we find the opportunity to explore different paths to the Divine. It's a reminder that, at our core, we are spiritual beings on a human journey, and our individual paths are converging into the same river of universal truth.

We should embrace open-mindedness in our spiritual pursuits, trusting in our capacity to do our best and recognizing that the essence of God resides within us all. It's a reminder that love, compassion, and understanding should be the guiding principles of our spiritual journey, for they are the bridges that connect us to one another and to the divine source of all creation.

In the end, "Pray for the dead" takes on a profound meaning. It becomes a practice that not only aids our departed loved ones on their journey but also connects us to human experience and spirituality. It is a reminder that, in our quest for meaning and connection, we should hold fast to love, open-mindedness, and the belief that, ultimately, we are all one.

In existence, we are threads interwoven, each one essential to the whole. The truth of our interconnectedness is a spiritual revelation that transcends boundaries of religion, culture, and creed. We are not isolated islands but rather interconnected souls sharing this earthly journey. To recognize this unity is to understand that the well-being of one is linked to the well-being of all. In this shared human experience, our duty is clear: to look out for each other, to extend a hand in times of need, to offer love and compassion as freely as the air we breathe. For in embracing our oneness, we find the path to a more harmonious and compassionate world and praying or thinking of the ones who passed on before us can only help them to be where they are meant to be.

HELPING LOVED ONES PASS AWAY

Elisabeth Kübler-Ross was a Swiss-American psychiatrist who revolutionized the way we understand the emotional and psychological experiences of individuals facing their own mortality. In her groundbreaking book "On Death and Dying" published in 1969, she introduced what have become known as the "Five Stages of Grief" or the "Kübler-Ross Model." These stages represent a framework to help understand the emotional responses that individuals may go through when confronted with a terminal diagnosis or the death of a loved one. It's important to note that not everyone goes through all of these stages, and they may not occur in a specific order. Here are the five stages:

1. **Denial:** In the initial stage, individuals often struggle to come to terms with the reality of their situation. They may deny the diagnosis or the impending death, believing that there must be some mistake. Denial serves as a psychological defense mechanism to buffer the shock of the news.

2. **Anger:** As the emotional numbness of denial wears off, it's common for individuals to experience intense anger. They may feel a sense of unfairness, resentment, or frustration about their situation. This anger can be directed at healthcare providers, family members, or even at the situation itself.

3. **Bargaining:** In this stage, individuals may attempt to make deals or bargains in a desperate attempt to change their circumstances. They may promise to change their behavior,

seek alternative treatments, or make deals with a higher power in exchange for more time or a different outcome.

4. **Depression:** Depression is a natural response to the impending loss or the reality of a terminal illness. It involves feelings of sadness, despair, and hopelessness. It's important to note that clinical depression can occur during this stage and may require professional intervention.

5. **Acceptance:** The final stage represents a state of coming to terms with the reality of the situation. Individuals begin to understand that their time is limited, and they seek to make the most of it. This stage doesn't necessarily mean happiness or a desire for death but rather an acknowledgment of the inevitable and a readiness to face it with as much peace and grace as possible.

It's crucial to understand that these stages are not linear, and individuals may move back and forth between them. Additionally, not everyone experiences all five stages, and the intensity and duration of each stage can vary widely among individuals. The Kübler-Ross Model has been influential in providing a framework for understanding the emotional complexities of facing death, but it's important to remember that grief and coping with mortality are deeply personal experiences.

It's a topic that many of us would rather avoid, but it's a reality we all eventually face: the end of life. When a loved one is nearing the final chapter of their journey, it becomes our responsibility and privilege to ensure that they pass away with the dignity and respect they deserve. Let's have an open and compassionate conversation about how we can do just that.

First and foremost, it's crucial to understand that the journey towards the end of life is deeply personal and unique for each individual. No two experiences are the same, and there is no one-size-fits-all approach to helping our loved ones through this transition.

It's essential to be empathetic and attentive to their emotional and physical needs. Some may want to discuss their feelings and fears openly, while others might prefer to keep their thoughts to themselves. The key is to be present and available, ready to support them in whatever way they need.

One of the most significant gifts we can offer our loved ones is the opportunity to express their wishes and preferences. Open and honest conversations about their end-of-life preferences can help ensure that their wishes are respected. This includes discussing topics such as:

Medical decisions: What are their preferences regarding medical treatments, interventions, and resuscitation?

Hospice care: Would they prefer to receive hospice care at home or in a specialized facility?

Funeral arrangements: What are their wishes for their final arrangements, including burial or cremation, and any specific religious or cultural customs?

Legacy and farewells: Are there messages they want to convey to family and friends, or any unfinished business they wish to address?

Initiating these conversations can be difficult, but it is an act of love and respect. It ensures that their final wishes are honored and can provide them with a sense of peace.

Pain management and ensuring physical comfort are crucial aspects of helping our loved ones pass away with dignity. Consult with healthcare professionals and palliative care teams to ensure that pain and discomfort are minimized. This includes managing symptoms, providing medication as needed, and making adjustments to their living space to maximize comfort.

As loved ones near the end of life, they may experience a wide range of emotions, including fear, sadness, and anxiety. Providing emotional support through active listening, empathetic conversations, and the presence of friends and family can be incredibly comforting. Encourage them to share their thoughts and feelings and be a compassionate and non-judgmental presence.

Helping our loved ones pass with dignity also involves celebrating their life and preserving their memories. Encourage them to reminisce and share stories from their life's journey. Create opportunities for them to connect with family and friends, either in person or through technology, so they can savor moments of love and connection.

Perhaps the most significant gift we can offer our loved ones during this time is the gift of our presence. Spend quality time with them, whether it's sharing a meal, listening to their favorite music, or simply sitting together in silence. Being there, physically and emotionally, reassures them that they are not alone on this final part of their journey.

Helping loved ones pass away with dignity is a profound act of love and compassion. It involves open communication, pain management, emotional support, and the preservation of cherished memories. Above all, it is about being there for them, ensuring that they feel respected, loved, and at peace as they take their final steps. While it is a difficult and emotional journey, it is one filled with opportunities for connection and profound moments of love and grace.

WRITE YOUR OWN OBITUARY

The notion of writing one's own obituary might strike some as morbid or unsettling. After all, it forces us to confront the inevitable—the end of our earthly journey. Yet, it is precisely in this act of composing our own obituary that we find a profound opportunity for introspection, self-discovery, and a deeper appreciation for life itself.

My late little brother, Jack, a nurse and a teacher of advanced first aid and courses for the American Red Cross, had an unconventional approach to teaching his students. He asked them to write their own obituaries. At first, I found the idea peculiar, even a bit unsettling. But Jack was onto something that transcended the ordinary.

The act of writing one's own obituary compels us to confront our mortality head-on. It forces us to contemplate the sum total of our existence—the joys, the sorrows, the triumphs, and the regrets. It challenges us to consider the legacy we wish to leave behind, and in doing so, it grants us a unique perspective on life itself.

As I observed Jack's students engage in this exercise, he witnessed transformations. Initially, some felt uncomfortable or even resistant to the idea. But as they delved into the task, they began to see its value. Writing their own obituaries made them consider their lives from a different vantage point. It prompted them to reflect on the impact they had on others and the goals they had yet to achieve.

It was through this process that many of them realized the importance of living authentically and purposefully. They recognized the significance of pursuing their passions, nurturing their relationships, and making a positive difference in the lives of others.

For years, like many, I had held back my emotions, fearing vulnerability and embarrassment. I had become adept at shielding my innermost feelings from the world. But when I wrote my own obituary, something remarkable happened. It was as if a floodgate had been opened, allowing a rush of real emotions to flow freely.

I came to understand that expressing our emotions, both joyous and sorrowful, is an essential part of the human experience. It connects us with our own humanity and with the humanity of others. It allows us to forge deeper connections, offer solace and support, and find a profound sense of release and healing.

Writing your own obituary is not an exercise in dwelling on death, but rather a celebration of life. It offers a unique opportunity to assess our accomplishments, our unfulfilled aspirations, and the relationships that have shaped us. It encourages us to take a closer look at the legacy we are crafting with every passing day.

In facing our own mortality, we are reminded that life is a precious and finite gift. It prompts us to live more authentically, to nurture our relationships, and to strive for our dreams with unwavering determination. It encourages us to open our eyes to our own destiny and embrace it with purpose and gratitude.

So, embrace the unconventional wisdom of writing your own obituary. It might just be the key to unlocking a deeper appreciation for life, a richer understanding of your own journey, and the courage to live your most authentic and meaningful existence.

CLOSING THOUGHTS

In the journey we've taken together, we've explored the depths of a single week that has the power to transform our lives. Along this path to happiness and spiritual awakening, there are invaluable lessons that resonate at the core of our existence.

Patience is the Key to a Good Life: Perhaps one of the most profound lessons is the importance of patience. It is the thread that weaves together the fabric of a good life. Patience teaches us to navigate the complexities of our human interactions with understanding and grace. It is the balm that soothes the wounds of misunderstanding and haste.

The Divine Essence of 'I Am': We've touched upon the idea that God is love, and within each of us resides a divine essence—'I Am.' This recognition invites us to connect with the profound source of love and goodness within ourselves and in every person we encounter. It reminds us that our thoughts and actions have the power to shape our reality.

The Essence of Prayer and Spirituality: Prayer, as we've come to understand it, is not confined to religious rituals; it is the act of putting positive intentions into the universe. Our thoughts and intentions have the ability to shape our reality, and in embracing this truth, we embark on a journey of spiritual awakening. Spirituality is an inner sanctuary of peace and strength, one that blossoms in the present moment.

Keeping Life Simple: As life unfolds before us, it's easy to become entangled in the web of complexity. Yet, simplicity is a virtue that calls us to focus on what truly matters. It encourages us to cherish the beauty of everyday moments and to cast aside the distractions that lead us astray.

The Wisdom of Years and Truth-Seeking: Time bestows upon us the gift of wisdom, a treasure that accumulates through our years and our pursuit of truth. Wisdom guides us to discern the profound from the superficial and to navigate life's challenges with resilience and grace.

Thoughts as Windows to the Soul: Our thoughts are not mere fleeting notions; they are the windows to our soul. They shape our words, and our words reveal the essence of our being. By paying attention to our thoughts, we gain insight into our true selves and the path we wish to forge.

Embracing Authenticity and the Present Moment: In closing, let us remember that authenticity is a sacred practice. It invites us to be unapologetically ourselves, free from the burden of external judgments. And as we've discovered, the present moment is where our lives truly unfold. It is the canvas upon which we paint our existence.

So, dear reader, as you continue your journey through life, may you carry these lessons in your heart. Embrace patience, nurture your spirituality, and live authentically in the present moment. Your life is a beautiful tapestry waiting to be woven, and with each passing day, you have the power to shape it into a masterpiece of happiness, purpose, and love.

ABOUT THE AUTHOR

We hope you enjoyed the journey through the pages of "Life in a Week" 2nd edition - A Journey to Happiness and Spiritual Awakening, as we introduced you to the humble mind behind this transformative book: Michael Shawn Keller.

Michael was born and raised in the charming suburbs of Connecticut, where the backdrop of his childhood was painted with the vibrant hues of a close-knit, amazing family. It was in this nurturing environment that he first developed his passion for storytelling, a talent that would blossom into a lifelong pursuit of enlightenment and self-discovery.

In 2009 and 2010, Michael ventured into the world of writing with his groundbreaking "Life in a Week" book series, a two-part exploration of happiness and spirituality. These works laid the foundation for his deep dive into these subjects and set the stage for his latest book. The second edition of "Life in a Week" brings these two facets of life together in an updated and integrated way that is simple and easy to read.

Michael's life has been a remarkable spiritual odyssey, an exploration of the multifaceted highs and lows of existence. Through the ups and downs of life, he has delved into every corner of human experience, emerging not only wiser but also with a unique ability to translate profound wisdom into relatable words.

Aside from his "Life in a Week" series, Michael has penned two other impactful books: "Bullies Among Us" and "Room 308." These books serve as guides for readers navigating the treacherous waters of bullying, shedding light on the importance of understanding and overcoming these challenges. "Room 308" holds a special place in Michael's heart as his first foray into fiction. In this touching tale, he gently guides readers through the journey of coming out as gay, a personal narrative that Michael courageously embarked upon in his 40s.

In his personal life, Michael has found love in its most radiant form. He is joyfully married to his remarkable partner, Jonathan, and together they share the blessing of a young son. Their union is a testament to the power of love, acceptance, and resilience.

Michael and Jonathan are not only partners in love but also partners in entrepreneurship. Their dynamic energy and innovative thinking have led them to embark on exciting entrepreneurial ventures, cementing their legacy as a power couple ready to make a positive impact on the world through compassion and love.

With "Life in a Week" 2nd edition - A Journey to Happiness and Spiritual Awakening, Michael Shawn Keller invites you to join him on a profound voyage of self-discovery and transformation. His words inspire, uplift, and guide you towards a life filled with happiness and spiritual awakening, just as he has experienced throughout his incredible journey.

www.ingramcontent.com/pod-product-compliance
Lightning Source LLC
Chambersburg PA
CBHW071330140726
47996CB00005B/1903